PROLOGUE

I HAVE DERIVED all of the material contained in *Dominic's Daughter* from reams of handwritten notes my mother left behind and from the memory of countless tales she related to me and the rest of her children over the years. Ruth Hogan, the granddaughter of Irish immigrants, was born in 1902. *Dominic's Daughter* is the account of her growing up in her grandmother's boarding house for laborers and sailors in a small town in northernmost Michigan. Dedicated to my mother, Ruth Hogan Thomas, this book is the fulfillment of a promise made to her years ago. This is her story; I've used her voice to tell it.

Dominic's Daughter is an account of people struggling to survive in a place where old farming skills are of no help, where nothing is convenient or easy, where food never stretches far enough, where children go to work at age twelve, boys laboring on the ore docks or in the mines, girls cleaning hotels and inns far from home in dangerous settings. For all of its brutal candor, though, *Dominic's Daughter* is an uplifting tale told with generous humor, the Irish secret weapon to cut trouble down to size. It is also a tribute to human courage, the kind required of all immigrants who have come and still come to America looking for a more decent way of life.

—Barbara Mullen

CHAPTER I

My Papa the Train Robber

M Y PAPA, DOMINIC Hogan, was a train robber. Not a very good one, but still a train robber. The Hogan family dispensed with the robbery as if it were an unpreventable accident or a bit of bad luck, but then, the Hogans were notoriously adept at excusing rambunctious behavior. The other side of my family, my Mama's folks, gave no leeway to such transgressions, particularly if a Hogan was involved.

The train robbery is a case in point. Far be it from my mama's family to have considered this unfortunate choice on Papa's part to be a momentary lapse of good judgment. I'm not defending Papa's youthful, if misguided, exuberance, but as far as I know nobody's ever told his side of the story. An accumulation of circumstances turned my papa into an outlaw; he didn't jump out of bed one morning with a sudden yearning to rob a railroad.

Papa's humble origins had called for a certain amount of creativity from the start. His parents,

my paternal grandpa and grandma, Edward Hogan and Eileen Doherty, had crossed the Atlantic
Ocean in separate ships from Ireland to Canada in
1875. They met and married soon afterward in Ontario, and migrated to the United States in 1882,
their wagon packed with a few worldly goods, mea-
ger supplies and two young sons.

Entering the United States through Northern Michigan, they first settled in Grand Marais,
a thriving lumber town on the shores of Lake Superior. Edward leased a small all-purpose grocery
store and wrote his younger brother Denny, still
in Ireland, inviting him to join them. Before long,
Denny arrived and got himself a job managing the
liveliest, most profitable saloon in Grand Marais.
So far, so good, until Dominic, Edward and Eileen's
third son, was born in 1884 just as the bottom fell
out of the lumbering business. Naturally, no one
blamed the birth of the infant for the slide in lumber sales, but the two events were always remembered together as if there was a certain connection.
As a consequence, Dominic himself believed from
childhood that his birthday had brought a curse on
the family, causing them to sell their general store
and move again.

Edward and Eileen Hogan, with their two boys,
baby Dominic and all their belongings piled into
their horse drawn wagon again, this time heading
toward Marquette, a booming iron ore and mining port a hundred miles west on Lake Superior.
Although when they got there there were plenty
of jobs to be had on the iron ore boats and on the
docks, the wages weren't enough to support three

growing boys and their three additional babies born during the next few years.

As a consequence, as soon as they each turned thirteen, Dominic and his two older brothers had to quit school and take any labor work they could find. At seventeen, personable affable Dommy, as Dominic was called, somehow landed a job sorting mail at the South Shore Railroad depot. That evening his father slapped him on the shoulder saying, "Congratulations, son, at last someone in this family has found respectable work."

Who could have known that this "respectable work" would bring nothing but bad luck to Dommy? Not so for his dashing twenty year old brother, Edward Jr., however. Dommy had been on his new job just six months when Edward Jr. showed up at the train depot one afternoon. Immediately eying a large burlap bag tightly wound in leather straps lying inside the mailroom on the linoleum floor, Edward gasped, "And what would that be, Dommy?"

"South Shore payroll bag. Just arrived for safe-keeping overnight," Dommy answered.

"Safekeeping where?" wheezed Edward.

Dommy, wanting to impress his big brother with his knowledge of the railroad business, told him, "A safe in the engineer's compartment on the train to Duluth leaving in the morning."

Edward whisked the cap off his slicked down brown wavy hair and slapped it to his heart. "Whew," he whistled through the space between his two front teeth while trying to reassemble his brainwaves to adjust to this unexpected, but golden, opportunity. Clapping a hand to Dommy's shoulder, mouth a second ahead of his thoughts, Edward stuttered. "Our ship has just come in, Dommy!"

"What ship you talking about?" Dommy asked numbly, having already switched his thoughts to the fresh bread and butter and a couple of ginger snaps in his lunch bucket.

"All you have to do, Dommy, is unlock the safe when you leave tonight. Nothing to it, kid. I'll do the rest."

"Nah, they would know it was me," Dommy said. "Have you become an idjut overnight, or were you always one?"

"How would they know? Plenty of people must know how to open that safe. I always thought you had some imagination, brother." Edward grabbed Dommy's hand priming it up and down like a water pump. "We're a team, kid," he gushed. "I'll be back at midnight." He sprinted out the back door, cheeks ruby red with excitement.

Dommy slid his long lanky frame onto a bench in the waiting room for a few minutes to contemplate his alternatives. He was afraid to do the deed, but more scared of his big brother's scorn if he refused. At suppertime he opened his lunch pail but his morning breakfast was having an argument with his stomach. He had no appetite for the lovely fresh bread he'd looked forward to earlier. Wanting to think otherwise, experience told Dommy that his brother, always chasing after an easy buck, would certainly appear at midnight. Now and then, though, for only a second or two, Dommy stopped sorting mail, smiled and wondered how much money that bag held and what he might do with his half. But a second later, heart pounding inside his ribcage, he went out to the waiting room and sank into the the smooth wooden bench again.

At midnight, Dommy answered Edward's knuckles at the door. Edward's eyes dancing like fireflies in the dark, he shoved past Dommy into the mailroom and asked, "All set? Hand me those keys, little brother."

"I ain't gonna do this," grunted Dommy, but Edward grabbed Dommy's key ring from his hand and headed toward the back door and the dark empty train. Dommy trailed behind him, scouring the platform for signs of movement and trying not to pass out from the terror of what was about to happen. Edward leaped into the engineer's compartment at the back of the engine, then reappeared in the doorway ten minutes later, sack in hand ready to depart the train.

"Jaysus, Edward, ya didn't have time to lock the safe behind ya, did ya?" Dommy hissed in the dark.

"Yah, I better check it again," Edward said dropping the bag on the coupling between two cars and swinging back into the engineer's compartment. Dommy crossed himself, begging the Lord's forgiveness as Edward picked up the bag again and leaped to the platform.

Dommy dashed back into the depot to lock the mailroom and the front door to the waiting room. In the meantime, Edward, bag over his back, had already made off down a side street from the rear of the depot.

Dommy, only yards behind him, feet flying, chased him clear to the outskirts of town with Edward turning to growl every block or so, "Go back, dimwit. You have to be there in the morning. Now they'll know it's you!"

"They'll know if I'm there, too," Dommy said, feet still peddling speedily behind Edward through the back streets and toward the woods.

Trudging west over rugged hills and wooded terrain, they never stopped running for three solid days till they reached the Copper Country Peninsula that juts out into Lake Superior.

By then, news of the train robbery had reached law officers across Michigan's Upper Peninsula. On the third day, a posse surrounded the two inept, ill-fated train robbers where they slumbered peacefully beneath an oak tree on a soft bed of underbrush. Handcuffed and arrested on the spot by the local sheriff and his deputies, they were hauled off to jail in the nearby town of Houghton.

Although heroes at first, the sheriff's staff was soon under fire for not capturing the money along with the robbers, a fact they were hard pressed to explain. Rumors multiplied, most supporting the theory that there was something fishy about that, as well as what followed later.

Dommy, the only one who confessed, became the only one convicted and the only one sentenced at a much publicized trial. He got one year in Marquette State Prison, a grim facility surrounded on one side by Lake Superior and on the other three sides by dense forest. Serious offenders such as

Black Bart and the like, had been incarcerated there earlier. The Hogans protested that placing a seventeen year old in such company was pretty drastic for a first time train robber, but to no avail.

Those who knew the Hogan brothers concluded that big brother Ed, figuring that a minor would get only one year, whereas he, himself, would have gotten more, had smooth-talked his kid brother into being the fall guy. Unfortunately, as soon as Dommy was safely in his cell, Edward disappeared like fog on a sunny day. Months flitted by before the family got word that fleet-footed Eddie had ended up in Minnesota. As news of his improved style of living there reached Marquette, the Hogan's deduced that he and the loot had traveled to Minneapolis on the same train. A couple of years later, the northland grapevine reported that brother Edward had invested the entire booty in oil stocks that had increased at a heretofore unheard of rate.

Edward, Mr.Lucky, as he was now referred to in the family, came to Marquette once driving a yellow Pierce Arrow touring car in 1914 and took me for a ride with the canvas roof down. He was about thirty-five then, dressed in a three piece suit and looking like a city dandy. I was a skinny twelve year old wearing a homemade pink cotton pinafore, my mop of auburn hair gathered at the back of my neck with a white satin ribbon. I knew nothing about how my Uncle Eddie had got his money, but I did think it strange that a Hogan could have any. I guess I was too captivated by his good looks and charm, even more than by his car, to worry about the money mystery.

He took me to an ice cream parlor on Washington Street where we sat at a marble table and talked over old times. Him, not me. At my age, I didn't have that many. Uncle Eddie looked me straight in the eye. "Can you swim, Ruthie?" he asked me.

I didn't want to insult him, so I tried to give him a polite answer to a silly question. Everybody who could walk a few blocks to the lake knew how to swim. "Oh, yes, I can swim," I said.

"I asked because your father was a champion swimmer as a boy. Maybe you didn't know that. Dommy used to dive off a rock near the ore docks and swim all the way around Presque Isle," Edward said, flashing his now straightened teeth at me to let me know he was ever so proud of his younger brother. I figured later that this visit had been about the time my father, the former convict, was having trouble finding a job anywhere.

But I'm getting ahead of myself. When my father got out of prison at eighteen, a year after the robbery, the railroad, surprisingly, gave him another job, this time as a freight brakeman. The Hogans reasoned that the officials were sympathetic to Dommy because they knew who had planned the robbery and profited by it. After three years, however, when Dommy hadn't received a normal promotion to conductor, each member of the Hogan family had developed a sympathetic theory as to Dommy's lack of advancement. My pretty dark haired, fair skinned mother, who at seventeen, had married Dommy a couple of years after he was released from prison, surprised everyone with her own explanation. "His love affair with Old John Barleycorn began the day he walked out of prison," she said. "And that's what did him in. Easy going Dommy was never the same after serving time."

A few years after Dommy had started back with the railroad, the train master paid my mama a visit one afternoon. I must have been about two then, and the three of us were living in a one bedroom rented apartment near the station. Mama was so sure Dommy was about to be fired that her hands trembled as she poured tea for his boss. Mr. Carlson, looking official in his blue and gray South Shore train master's uniform, took a few sips before getting to the real purpose of his visit. "Barbara," he said, "we have to get Dommy away from his drunken ruffian friends here in town." Setting down his cup, he paused a moment. "I'm going to give him one more chance. I've talked the South Shore Railroad into switching Dommy's run to Duluth. You'd have to move there, of course. But that's the best I can do."

"Thank you for your thoughtfulness," Mama said, feeling genuinely grateful to the man. "That'll be fine. We'll start packing tomorrow."

Mama drank the remainder of the pot after the train master had left, reciting a silent prayer with each cup.

We lived in a residential hotel in downtown Duluth for several months and Mama seemed happier. We had a hot plate stove and miniature sink and a small table and chairs at one end of a living room. I slept on a sofa and Mama and Papa had a separate little bedroom. Papa came straight home from work every night in time for the supper Mama had cooked. During the day Mama and I walked through a nearby park to a small grocery store and got home just in time to boil potatoes and a vegetable and to fry sausages for our evening meal.

All the while, Papa kept calling his brother Edward in Minneapolis and leaving messages with his brother Edward's wife Doris. Papa had believed from the day we arrived in Minnesota that Edward would take this opportunity with us nearby to pay him his share of the loot from the robbery. But Edward never called him back from Minneapolis and one morning Papa announced that he would never phone him again. That evening he didn't show up for supper and Mama and I ate alone.

Before long, Dommy had found himself a whole new set of drinking companions to share a pint with after work. By the time he returned to our hotel room at night, he had turned mellow, saying funny things to Mama and carrying me around on his shoulders. One night he taught me to dance the jig. "Come on, Ruthie. Dance with Papa," he said, blue eyes lighting up his face. "Hold your body stiff. Get on your toes. Swing your legs." When I fell to the floor, he picked me up and swung me around like a kite. Another night he sang "Danny Boy" for Mama and me. I was sure he had to be the tallest, most handsome, curly headed tenor singer in America. When he finished the song, Mama walked over to him and kissed him on the cheek and he kissed her back on the lips. And then I heard him say, "I love you, Barbara."

But, alone in the room the next day, Mama's spirits wilted. She told me later that she had already sensed that her Dommy might never recover from his brother's final rejection. And she wasn't the least surprised when the South Shore Railroad fired Papa a few months later.

Back in Marquette again, we rented a two-room apartment in a dilapidated building at the wrong end of Champion Street. Dommy found unskilled jobs, but couldn't stay sober long enough to keep them. Mama's father, William Wiseman, a no-nonsense decent man from Edinburg, Scotland, had been supporting the three of us until one day his patience ran out. Standing tall in his Sunday mass three-piece suit, heavy red hair brushed neatly to the side, he appeared unannounced at our door one afternoon when Papa was out. Marching into the tiny combination living room kitchen, he stood at the center of a worn rag carpet and issued an ultimatum to his daughter. "You have to leave him, Barbara," he stated. "I'm finished taking care of the lot of you."

I was three then, but I remember Mama's tears that evening and her nervous fingers brushing my tangled curls. "Ruthie," she said, "Mama has to decide if we should stay here with your papa or go to live with Grandma Bridget and Grandpa William."

I loved Papa but I hated seeing him sick so many mornings and having to bring him glasses of water in bed. And I wanted Mama to stop crying all the time, so I whispered to her, "Let's move in with Ma and Da until Papa gets better."

"I hope that happens," Mama said.

Grandpa William arrived the next morning and as soon as I saw him I felt safe. Lifting me up with one arm, he snatched Mama's suitcase from her with the other hand. And the three of us left without a word to Papa who was still snoring in the bedroom.

CHAPTER 2

Ma's House

As soon as we heard Papa's voice at the front door my eighteen- year-old Aunt Bessie threw her arms around my waist and hauled me up the hall stairs. I wrapped my legs around her middle, kicked her skinny butt and yanked at the braid down her back, but Mama's younger sister was almost as stubborn as my Grandma Bridget when she set her mind to something. Dragging me into her bedroom she shoved me onto the closet floor, then closed the door behind both of us. It was pitch black in there except for a slim crack of light beneath the door. "Hush up," she said holding her hand over my mouth.

I pulled hard on Bessie's arm trying to get loose. "I know that's my papa knocking at the door and I want to see him!"

"Shhh. Just be quiet," Bessie hissed into my ear. "Ma will kill me if your papa hears you yelling!"

I wanted to cry, but Mama and I had only been at Grandma Bridget's house a day and I didn't want Ma mad at me any more than Bessie did. With her hand still on my mouth, Bessie yanked me closer to her with her other arm. "Ma says three is too young to understand grown up business." We snuggled up together on the floor hardly breathing. I guessed Bessie was as scared as I was.

I heard the fist at the front door slam hard one last time and then stop and Bessie took her hand off my mouth. "Your papa must have left," she whispered and I pushed away from her, smacked open the closet door and ran for the stairs. Bessie tried to snatch the back of my dress, but I escaped her and flew down the stairs, then crumpled to the floor and started to sob when I couldn't reach the doorknob to open the front door.

Bessie dashed to the kitchen to get Ma. "Thank the Lord we got rid of him," Ma declared, frizzy brown hair wilder than usual, long legs sailing down the hall to meet her.

"I won't move!" I screamed through tears. I already hated Ma and everybody in that house except Mama and Da and that was a lot of people counting all Ma's boarders. How did they know? Maybe Papa had got well since the day before and had come for Mama and me.

Mama came back from an errand a few minutes later and Ma related what had happened like it was the best news since everyone came to America. "Thank God, he didn't take her with him," Mama exclaimed and Ma's right hand swung into the sign of the cross.

Right after that, my mother took her maiden name back to please Ma and Da, as we called

Grandpa William and Grandma Bridget. Ma and Da had decided to adopt me as well but their plan had a hitch in it. They had to get my papa's agreement to do it and by then, Papa had meandered south to Milwaukee or thereabouts and couldn't be located. Months later, when he finally resurfaced in Chicago, Papa flatly refused to sign the adoption papers. This left me with a mother using her maiden name and my being the only person at Ma's house with the name Hogan, a name Ma associated with hooligans, ruffians and worst of all, pigs in the parlor Irish.

The mystery of my name's origin wasn't a problem until my mama tried to enroll me in school when I turned four a year later. With no kindergartens in Marquette then, a four year old could attend the first grade for two years if the school gave permission; the second year was then called "real first grade." Anyway, Mama had to do some fast-talking to explain the Hogan name to the principal, who, according to Bessie's version, was finally convinced by Mama's big brown eyes. Mama said the poor man plainly was just too confused to question her story further.

To be sure that nothing went haywire at the last minute, Mama got up earlier than usual on my first day of school, finished her breakfast work at Ma's house, draped her best shawl around her shoulders, and marched me over to the four room red sandstone schoolhouse a few blocks away.

"I think I'm scared, Mama," I said. "What if they don't want me?"

Mama squeezed my hand. "Don't be silly, Ruthie Hogan. They're lucky to have you."

"Here comes your teacher," Mama said as we opened the schoolhouse door. I dove behind Mama's skirt for fear the beautiful lady floating toward us would disappear if I spoke. Miss Johnson was the closest thing to my idea of an angel, soft blond curls, rosebud lips, pink complexion, that I would ever meet.

I peeked at her from behind the fold of Mama's skirt, then poked my face out to get a better look. And to my surprise, Miss Johnson picked up my hand in hers and said, "Let me take you to your classroom, Ruthie."

At Ma's, nobody seemed to own me and yet everybody bossed me, but Miss Johnson made me feel in charge of myself. When we reached the classroom she gave me a desk of my very own smack in front of hers. Except for the red sandstone blocks at the front, the schoolhouse was more or less an enlarged shack but I thought it was grand and clean, with plants on the shelves near the cloak closet and a potted geranium decorating Miss Johnson's desk. I slid into my seat and ran my fingertips over the paper, pencils and large letters of the entire alphabet cut out on a card in front of me. I was so excited to trace the letters for Miss Johnson that I almost forgot to wave goodbye to Mama.

The poorest sections of our town were at the extreme north and south ends. Our house was as close as you could get to the south end without being in the south end, a few blocks north of the railroad tracks that were the dividing line. The far south side beyond the tracks was called Shantytown by a lot of people. Grades one through three for all of south Marquette including Shantytown were housed in my school.

I came back from lunch on my third day of school and found all the kids standing in the street and a police wagon parked out front. Miss Johnson instructed her first graders to gather around her. "Just pretend I'm the old woman in the shoe," she said smiling.

We four and five year olds giggled and held hands and Miss Johnson made it seem like a game. In a nice calm voice she explained to us that Michael O'Falvey, who was nine years old and still in the first grade, had come back from lunch drunk. "He's only being rambunctious, so don't you worry," she told us. "A few broken windows is all. The police will be bringing him down to the station as soon as they can manage to get handcuffs on him."

I loved Miss Johnson more than ever after that day for telling us the truth about Michael instead of some faked up story. I ran the three blocks to school every morning after that so I wouldn't miss anything exciting at the other end. Ma and Mama kept asking me if I was afraid of this or that at school. "Not a bit," I told them over and over. They said I was "a brave little girl" but the truth is, compared to Ma's house where nobody ever broke one of Ma's iron clad rules, going to school was almost as much fun as the county fair in August.

At the time, Ma and Da, one uncle, two aunts, my mother and me, and six to eight boarders lived at Grandma Bridget's. Mama and I had been at Ma's about a year when my two-year-old cousin Jeanette joined us as well. Jeanette's mother, Aunt Annie, another of Ma's daughters, and oldest sister to Mama and Bessie, had just died from some kind of pleurisy. Annie's husband, Colin, the baby's father, left Jeanette with Ma, saying he'd be back for her "as soon as he got on his feet again."

His feet, however, didn't get him back to Ma's house for seven years, not until Jeanette was nine and he had married again. Nobody criticized Jeanette's papa; in fact, Ma and Mama and Bessie often praised him while cleaning the supper dishes. "Colin's a good man to send Jeanette presents and pay for the food she eats," I heard Ma say one night. "A man has no way to take care of a child until he has another wife, does he?" Bessie and Barbara, my mama that is, agreed, but then that didn't count; they always agreed with Ma in her presence.

The talk about Jeanette's papa got me wondering what Ma would have said if Mama had dropped me off and not returned for seven years. I was pretty certain that Ma wouldn't have been praising Mama the way she praised Colin. She might have sent me to that awful orphanage out of town they often talked about. How did I know? Nobody really knew what Ma might do from day to day. When I got too stirred up about this possibility, I made myself remember stories I'd heard about all the other urchins Ma had taken in before me and had kept indefinitely.

As for the boarders, Ma had to take them in after Da lost three fingers in a lumber mill accident six years before Ma and I moved in. The company gave him a different job stoking the boiler and he was glad, but it paid much less than his old foreman's job. Fortunately, he and Ma had bought a good size house when they first married and since then, had added some lean-tos making the place quite large for our part of town.

From a porch facing the street, an entrance led into a hall that ran the length of the house; a front banister staircase led upstairs to the bedrooms. At the front end of the first floor was a parlor that Ma used only for guests and for special occasions. The next doorway off the hall opened to a sitting room that turned into a bedroom for Da and Ma at night. Ma claimed it was the only place she and Da could have any privacy from the menagerie upstairs. And believe me, no one *dared* to knock on that door after nine P.M.

Further down the hall, we entered a large dining room where everyone, all the borders and family, ate breakfast and supper. And, through an archway, we came into Ma's spacious kitchen with its icebox, woodstove, washtub sink and a pantry.

A rear stairwell off the kitchen took us upstairs to five bedrooms. Four boarders and Uncle Danny, Ma's youngest son, occupied the largest room of all at the rear; the second room, a tiny bedroom. was reserved for the boarder who could afford to pay for a private room. Bessie and little Jeanette shared the third room so Bessie could take care of Jeanette, but Mama and I had the very best room of all at the front of the house with a wide window that faced a veranda below where Ma kept a lovely flower garden every summer.

The backyard was my favorite place. Whenever I finished my chores I snuck out there to be by myself. Ducking under the clothes reel, running past the wood shed, I dashed into the barn to visit with our horse Charlie and our cow Gracie in their stalls. We had long conversations; I told them my secrets, what I thought about each and every person in Ma's house, who I could trust, who smelled bad, who had been mean to me that day. And usually at the end I said how much I missed Papa and wondered when I would ever see him again. They listened and snorted and mooed back at me and then I went into the carriage room on the other side of the barn and climbed the ladder to the loft and jumped in the hay and hooted and hollered for about fifteen minute.

On my way back to the house, I usually made a stop in the outhouse. We had a sturdy brick outside, wood inside, two-seater. The women cleaned the place everyday after emptying the slop jars from under the beds and wash bowls on the nightstands. Still, I did my business in a hurry while trying not to breath. Besides the stink, it was dark and scary in there, the only light coming from a small star and a moon carved near the top of the door that told people our outhouse was for both men and women. Eventually, Ma installed a flush toilet in the house cellar and a bathtub at one end of the dining room, but that was several years later.

Cleaning up after everyone, feeding everyone and doing laundry for everyone required all the help Ma could round up. Mama, at twenty-three, Bessie, at nineteen, and Ma, who was about forty-eight then, worked seven days a week. The day I turned five I was given chores too, to dry the dishes, set the long dining table and rip sheets off the beds once a week. Jeanette, being only three then, was still too young for Ma's army. Ma paid my mother eight dollars a month, plus our room and board, for fourteen hours of labor a day. I guess Mama had no choice. There weren't many jobs other than housekeeping for women any place else in town. I rubbed her neck at night when she crawled into bed bone tired. "Never mind, Ruthie, we're lucky to have a roof over our heads," she told me at least once a week.

A lot of things confused me at Ma's, but one of them was never about who ruled the roost. Grandma Bridget was to be obeyed by all who entered. I resented that rule from the day we moved in. I had a mama of my own in the house, but Mama practically saluted when Ma yelled, "March!" It shamed me to have my mother treated like another kid in the house. By the end of that first year at Ma's house, I had crossed Mama off as someone who would ever stand up to Ma.

I often heard Mama and Bessie talking in Bessie's bedroom at night. One night Mama said, "I married too young, I suppose, and had Ruthie too soon." Another time, I heard Mama crying. "If only Dommy hadn't served time in that terrible prison. I know he felt degraded by that, but he never talked about it. I asked him questions that he shrugged off. Otherwise, he was so fun loving and kind. If only he had let me help him instead of burying his shame and anger in the drink."

"He broke your heart, Barbara," Bessie said. "Don't forget."

I didn't understand all that had happened between Mama and Papa, but I believe Mama loved him because I saw the sadness in her eyes when people said bad things about him.

I know I should have felt grateful to Ma like Mama said. I could have saved myself a lot of trouble by tiptoeing around the house and pretending to be invisible. But staying out of sight and quiet was not my nature. Everybody, boarders and family alike, ranted about "my constant jabbering and non-stop movement." After supper one night, one of the boarders offered me a nickel to be still and silent for five minutes.

"Watch me. I can do it," I said. I wanted to prove something to this particular boarder who was nothing but a snake in the grass. I got goose bumps every time his squinty eyes looked in my direction. I plunked myself down on a dining chair flattening a hand on each knee to hold my wiggling legs still. Then bit down hard on my tongue to keep any sound from slipping out between my teeth.

I felt myself getting hot, then burning up, then ready to explode. My forehead grew sweaty; I couldn't get enough air through my nose to breathe. At that moment, the devil entered my body, and, lifting me from my chair, shot me upward into a standing position. I screamed like I'd been sitting on hot coals and shoved myself away from the table. Knocking over my chair, I made a dash for the hall. Before tearing up the stairs, I swung around and stuck out my tongue at the stingy old leech. Yelling hysterically the whole time, I bolted up the back stairs to my room and hid on the closet floor behind Mama's clothes, hoping Ma wouldn't find me to give me a whipping.

I sat on the top step later and listened to Bessie and Mama who were doing the kitchen cleanup below me. "Don't tell me she's going to be hysterical like Bertha," Bessie said. Connecting me to Aunt Bertha, my papa's sister, or any of the Hogans, was always bad news. For a while I thought maybe being a Hogan meant I'd inherited a disease, or an addled brain or a cursed soul. But I had already resolved that I'd rather be a bloomin' idjut and happy, than be a smart old grouch like some people I knew. From what I had heard about the Hogans, they enjoyed life a lot more than anybody at Ma's house. Besides, I had something else percolating in my brain that night: I had to get even with Squinty Eyes. I had no shortage of ideas, but most of them would have got me a free paddy ride to the slammer so I decided to sleep on it.

The next day a brilliant plan came to me while Miss Johnson was teaching us the stupidest song I had ever heard. That night after supper, Squinty Eyes, sitting in the best-stuffed chair in the sitting room, picked up a hunting magazine and started to leaf through it. I let him get started on it good, stroking his wispy beard, licking his fingers to turn pages. Then I parked myself on a stool two feet to the side of him but where I could face him.

I opened my mouth wide as a baseball, and, at the top of my lungs, with a voice that usually made people wince, sang—and sang—and sang—and sang: *"A birdie with a yellow bill hopped upon my window sill . . ."* until the old snake lunged up out of his chair.

"Quiet!" he yelled.

But I kept right on: *"A birdie with a yellow bill hopped upon my window sill . . ."*

Fishing frantically into his vest pocket, he brought out a nickel, slapped it into the palm of my hand and screeched, "Jaysus, Mary and Joseph, girl. Shut up!"

Scooting upstairs two at a time, I fell on top of my bed face down. Pounding my fists into the pillow, I howled until my stomach ached. When I got down to giggling, I pulled out the nickel from my pinafore pocket. Caressing it tenderly, I polished it on my skirt, held it up to the light, planted a juicy kiss on my fingers holding it and tucked it under my pillow. I smiled, for the first time thinking: *Maybe these adults aren't quite as smart as they pretend they are.*

CHAPTER 3

Welcome Mr. Taft

I WAS SIX the summer of 1908 when Mr. Taft, "Mr. Republican," as Da called him, was running for a first term in the White House. Our town had been chosen to be one of his campaign stops during our combined Chautauqua Indian celebration and Fourth of July activities. With weeks of preparation, the town had been decorated one end to the other with flags and flowers and the Chautauqua had been set up in a tremendous tent on Longyear's Field at the foot of Ridge and Lake Shore Drive on the grass sloping down to Lake Superior.

On a rare windless day, the temperature reached eighty-five degrees, nearly ninety inside the tent. Although many speeches led up to the President's appearance, Da, my Grandpa, being a staunch Republican, wouldn't consider deserting his spot upfront to cool off outside. He had taken his suit coat off, but refused to remove his vest or to roll up his shirtsleeves. "Not with the next President of the United States of America about to stand before me to remind us that we're living in the best country on earth," he told Ma who was wiping beads of perspiration from his forehead with her handkerchief.

I had already seen the Indian craft tables, soft leather moccasins, colorful beaded purses and copper jewelry, and watched the Indian kids in their native suits and feather headdresses do their dances. But now I was dying to see all the game booths and charity bazaar counters set up by every church in town, and to eat corn on the cob at one of the lunch counters. The quarter Da had given me to spend as I wished was sizzling a hole in my pocket.

I jumped from one foot to the other for a while until Da let go of my hand for a second and I snuck over to the side of the tent and peeked through an opening half-heartedly. Then suddenly to my utter surprise, I spotted my mother walking past. Darting out through the opening, I scooted after her. "Mama, Mama," I called out, but she didn't turn around. I ran as fast as my legs let me and still couldn't catch her because of all the folks I had to dodge on the way. Next thing I saw was her laughing and chattering with three other people and one of them was Aunt Bessie. I hardly recognized either her or my mother, both looking pretty as pattern magazine models in new cotton dresses, ankle-length with lace trim at the collars, and wearing wide brimmed bonnets decorated with flowers.

What I saw then stopped me dead in my tracks and left my mouth gaping open. A gentleman in a Sunday best suit next to my mama set his hand on her shoulder without Mama spitting in his face or shoving him away. Instead, he cocked his head to the side and smiled at her as if she were a delicious chocolate sundae. Next thing I knew, the other man inched closer to Bessie and whispered something in her ear. Bessie pointed her finger at his nose and giggled. When the man near Mama glanced away for a second, Mama darted me a look over her shoulder; then, resting the back of one hand on her bum, wiggled her fingers faster than a concert pianist, motioning for me to go back to the tent.

So this was why she had ordered me to go to the celebration with Grandma and Grandpa and why Bessie had got a neighbor to watch Jeanette. I felt hurt and mad all at once and mixed up too. And what would Papa think about the way she was acting? I watched the four of them until they passed all the tents and the eating stands and game booths and were out of sight.

I didn't feel like going back to join Ma and Da. I roamed around by myself for a while until I spied Teresa, a school friend whose mother was working at one of the stands. I slipped my quarter from my pocket and showed it to Teresa to persuade her to join me, and we headed straight to the Candy Kitchen one block away.

As we licked the last of our ice cream from our spoons and sucked up every bubble at the bottom of our Green River drinks, I begged Teresa to go to Lakeside Park where the sports games were starting. We had watched some baseball, South Marquette against North Marquette, and some old guys throwing horseshoes, when Teresa whipped three fingers to her mouth and yelped, "Quelle heure et'il? I'd better beat it back to ma mere's stand or I'll catch the Devil even if Mr. Taft himself is waiting in line for one of her cotton cones."

I couldn't think of anywhere else to go by myself, so I headed back toward Ma's house. The sun had started to fade and my feet were burning. By the time I walked the ten blocks, I was relieved to see our white frame house on the corner, only I wasn't sure I could drag my legs up the porch steps.

Bessie croaked, "Ahhhhhh! She's here," when I pushed open the door and I knew I was in trouble.

Then my mother came running to the door. "Thank you, God. Thank you," she wailed while grabbing me by the collar and yanking me inside. "Where have you been? Are you crazy, or did you purposely decide to torment me and your grandparents and the rest of the family?" She rubbed her fingers over my face and through my tight curls and plastered her hands all over the rest of me to make sure the entire me had made it home, I guess.

"We've been hunting for you all over town," Bessie shrieked. "Ma organized a search posse of boarders and gave them orders to find you—or find another place to live." Just then Ma blasted in through the back door and raced down the hall. I shut my mouth so the ice cream and Green River in my stomach wouldn't explode onto Ma's good rag carpet. My body stiffened to get ready for a whipping I'd never forget, but when I snuck a peek at

Ma she was just leaning against the banister holding her head in her hands.

Then I noticed Da with the hall phone receiver dangling from his fingers. "I was just calling the police," he said, setting the receiver back in its cradle. As he started toward me I waited for his mustache to curl up in his usual smile, but instead, in a brand new stern voice he said, "You were inconsiderate, girl. You scared your mother and your grandmother half to death. And you disobeyed our rule about not meandering around town by yourself. Especially today. Lumberjacks and hayseeds and men off the reservation are all over town for the celebration." He rubbed his hands together furiously. "Never do such a foolish thing again! Do you hear me?" He shook his head; his beard and sandy red hair swayed back and forth like maybe they harbored their own separate grievances against me. "I'm disappointed in you, little girl," he said, then turned and walked away without another word.

I didn't care now what punishment I was given by Ma or Mama. When Ma sent me straight to bed with no dinner I made a dash for upstairs. I might still get an ear boxing tomorrow but I didn't care one way or the other. Nothing could be worse than having my grandpa mad at me. I loved my grandpa more than anybody in the world, almost as much as Papa. Every afternoon when Da came from work I'd sit in his lap while he asked me about school and called me his Bonnie Bairn and let me wind his beautiful silver watch on a chain. He had never before scolded me in a hard voice.

Later on, after the boarders had eaten their supper, I snuck down the upstairs hall to the stairwell and sat on the top step to listen to conversation from the kitchen. I smelled the sweetness of Da's pipe and then heard him let out a huge belly laugh. Then Ma and Bessie and Mama and Mama's brother, Danny, laughed uproariously too. "That'll teach you Barbara," Da said producing another big guffaw. "Not telling your date you'd been married. Acting like a happy go lucky single girl. And then having a six year old chase after you calling, "Mama! Mama!" They each took a turn teasing Mama and telling the story again and each time they howled louder than the last.

I was glad to hear them sounding happy but it made me think about Mama in a whole new way. I remembered how young and pretty she had looked that afternoon and it came to me just like that that Mama had a right to enjoy herself. My face in my hands, I leaned against the stairwell. I was sorry I had spoiled Mama's date, making her come home early to look for me. If I could do it again, I would stay put in that hot tent with Grandma and Grandpa even if I fainted dead away before Mr. Taft spoke. And tomorrow I would tell Mama that, for sure. And say I was sorry.

Da couldn't have been more pleased when William Taft won the election in November. The next day Ma and Da planned to celebrate the event with some friends of theirs who owned a tavern down by the docks. I couldn't imagine why they invited me to take the buggy ride with them, but I knew then they had forgiven me for worrying them after Mr. Taft's speech on the Fourth of July. I hollered, "You bet!" before they could change their minds. I wore my church dress, green wool with a polka dot collar, and a gray winter coat that had been Bessie's when she was my age. Around my neck, I tied a Kelly green scarf that Mama had knit me because she said green showed off my chestnut brown curls.

Sitting between Grandma and Grandpa as our horse Charlie trotted on ahead of us, clippity clopping through the streets where kids from school were playing and having to get out of our way, I pretended I was a little rich girl and my Da owned a copper mine and an iron ore mine and a lumber mill and that the whole family lived in a beautiful Victorian mansion on a street heading straight down to the lake. But I woke up when Da's old friend Jimmy Murphy's Irish pub near a loading dock on Lake Street came into view.

One half of Mr. Murphy's house contained the pub, the other half the family living quarters. Since women weren't allowed in the tavern, Ma and I went directly into the living room to visit with Mrs. Murphy while Da joined Mr. Murphy and the men in the saloon. We could hear them congratulating one another as though they had personally ushered President Taft into the White House.

A while later, Grandpa, grinning ear to ear, appeared at the door of the living room carrying a tray. Setting the tray on a tea table in front of Grandma and me, he leaned over and gave Ma's cheek a little pinch. "How are the ladies doing this fine afternoon?" he asked us.

"It's plain to see you're faring well, William," Ma answered.

"Sure I am," he agreed. Cheeks rosy, he strolled back and forth nattering away about the election, the state of the world, how fortunate we were to have a brand new President with good sense. He couldn't stop talking and I couldn't take my eyes off him. I'd never seen him a little tipsy before, which I guessed he was. He looked younger too, a clump of his bushy red hair flopping onto his forehead, dapper in his dark striped suit.

"I almost forgot why I came in here," he said lifting three cold glasses of sarsaparilla one by one from his tray. With a graceful flourish, he presented one to Grandma and one to Mrs. Murphy and one to me. Ma gazed adoringly above the top of her glass at her husband, eyes suddenly wide with tiny flecks of light shooting out from the centers.

As if Da pinching Ma's cheek hadn't been enough to make me swoon, now Grandma Bridget was offering Grandpa an outstretched hand. "Come here, William," she said. He took a few steps toward her, and, bending one knee to lower himself to the floor, placed both hands under her chin and kissed her on the lips. Dumbfounded and struck silent, I tried to absorb this amazing event. I never dreamed that two people forty some years old could be so romantic, especially when one of them was Ma.

I could have died happy that second sure in my soul that nothing in my lifetime could ever top this. I took a sip of my very first cold sarsaparilla and said a silent thank you, then and there, to Mr. Taft.

CHAPTER 4

Ma, Willie, and Me

MA'S HOUSE WASN'T so bad for the first few years. When I arrived I was a pretty three year old and loved by everyone, and, by the time I was seven, I had devised my own methods for dealing with Ma. First and foremost, I made myself look busy every minute. There was nothing Ma despised more than a person at rest. Second and third, I stayed out of her way as much as possible and never, never, sassed her back. No matter how much I grew to fear Ma's strict discipline, though, I understood that the family owed her a debt of gratitude.

She worried about our food supply night and day: Would it stretch until spring? Would the coming summer produce the needed vegetables for canning? Would the boarders bring in enough money to buy a side of beef? Would there be enough milk for the children to drink and for butter and for our coffee? How many hungry kids would there be at her table during the coming year?

Grandma Bridget used our house lot and also rented the lot next door for planting potatoes, turnips, parsnips and cabbages, and always one big pumpkin, to last through the year. "If you don't intend to starve, pitch in," Ma chanted while handing out work assignments each week. We girls and the adult women took turns picking off bugs from the potatoes in the garden four or five times a season. When it came time to dig up the potatoes, everybody got dirty hands. Ma stored her larder in our cellar, vegetable bins occupying one half of the entire area, about ten feet by ten feet in size. Starting at about age six, one of my jobs was to sit in this dark bin for two-hour periods pulling sprouts from the potatoes so they wouldn't rot. To pass time, I told myself stories and pretended I was somewhere else with the sun on my face.

Once a year Ma sent to Sears Roebuck for a barrel of apples and a keg of gingersnaps. After installing galvanized tin bins in the pantry, she was able to save money by purchasing flour and sugar and coffee wholesale. Although we lived next to a grocery store, we almost never bought canned goods or any other extra items. We did bring our own vinegar jug and kerosene can to the store for the owner, Jack Flynn, to fill up once a month. Ma paid her bill every two months, and each time she did, Mr. Flynn gave her a bag of fruit for a treat. "Oh, Mr. Flynn you shouldn't have," she'd say on each occasion, smiling shyly and ducking her head into her shoulder.

Mr. Flynn turned into a blushing old fool immediately. "But it was my pleasure, Bridget," he'd say, tugging at his vest bottom trying to hide his plump belly. I had to snap my hand to my mouth and duck behind an apple barrel to stop from having a fit of giggles the first time I saw Ma turn her charm on Mr. Flynn. I was soon impressed, however, with the fact that she never once left the store empty handed.

Around the first of November each year when the weather turned cold enough, Ma bought her side of beef and hung it out in our carriage room attached to the barn. One year, when money was more scarce than usual, she instead had the butcher cut up one of our pasture cows. I didn't touch beef all that winter. Ma fussed at me over supper every evening: "Eat that meat on your plate, girl. You're skinny as a rail."

Then one night seeing another slab of our cow on my plate, I looked Ma square in the face and stated, "The rest of you can be cannibals if you like, but I refuse." To everyone's astonishment, especially mine, Ma became silent throughout the meal and thereafter let me turn into a potato and vegetable eater for the rest of that year. I never guessed the word cannibal would put a hex on Ma, or I'd have used it sooner. You never knew with her; you just never knew.

Take what happened the first time she and I went raspberry picking together and she transformed herself into a person I enjoyed being with. My Uncle Danny drove a rural mail carrier route by horse and buggy, and every summer during the raspberry harvest season he took Ma and one of her daughters with him in the buggy and dropped them off ten miles out of town in the Skandia farm country to live with a Swedish family for a week. To my amazement, during the seventh summer of my life, Ma chose me instead of one her daughters to be her partner.

I was terrified to work side by side with Ma, but thank goodness I knew how to please her by then. All I had to do was work my bum off and she'd be smiling, or at least not growling. We picked those raspberries all day long, and on Uncle Danny's return trip to town after he'd delivered the mail, he would collect our filled tins. Then, before returning to the post office, he'd unload the fresh raspberries at Ma's house so Mama and Bessie could preserve them.

Nothing had prepared me for the change that would come over Ma out there in the sun away from the cooking, cleaning, laundry and gardening at home. Believe me, we did our quota of picking for our house every day and for the farmer's family as well, but at lunchtime Ma and I would sit under a tree and eat the sandwiches and drink the lemonade that Anna Larson, the farmer's wife, had prepared that morning. Using a Swedish accent, Ma told me story after story regarding people, some admirable, some idjuts, that Uncle Danny had met on his farm country mail route. I laughed whether I got the joke or not, cause it tickled me to see Ma having fun. Sometimes she roared so hard at her own stories I wondered if she was expelling laughter she'd stored up all year..

"Let's make some jars of thick jam when we get home and hide them in a corner of the cellar just for us," she said, poking me on my arm like we were girl friends instead of boss and slave. "We'll save it for our own private treats, Ruthie," she promised.

"Honest?" I said, appreciating what a treat that would be. We never ever made jam because jam took too much sugar and our sugar had to be saved for coffee and a special cake once in a great while. I'd never minded not having jam because the pure berry sauce that dripped through soft cotton rags was delicious, especially on toast. I didn't tell Ma that, though, because doing so would have spoiled our very first secret together.

Those days in the country were the nicest times I had ever spent with my Grandma Bridget. With the sunshine on her face, her flowered cotton skirt folded up to her knees, her long bare legs stretched out before her on the grass and a breeze blowing through her loose sandy colored hair, she seemed a young girl again. Each day at lunch I sat closer to her under our favorite oak tree with our backs resting on its trunk. On the last day, she put her arm around my shoulders as we talked, just as I'd been wishing she would all week. I guess if I could have, I'd have had that lunch hour last forever.

I don't know how long the warm feeling between Ma and me would have lasted if cousin Willie hadn't moved in the day after we returned from the country. I do know that Willie's presence altered our household from the day he walked through the front door. Willie was the kind of person—never mind he was only nine—who could make the very floor under your feet shift when you weren't look-ing.

I don't claim that Ma and I had no differences before Willie moved in, but Willie turned our clash of wills into another Civil War. Before Willie, I'd respected Ma's stubborn, single-minded efforts to keep everyone under her roof fed and safe. After Willie, I only had room in my heart for resent-ment toward Ma for her favoritism toward Willie. I guess that was wrong, but I couldn't seem to help myself.

Willie's father, Thomas Gummerson, a sec-ond generation Swede, smart, well educated and admired, was an engineer at the Lake Shore En-gineering Company. Willie's mother Nellie was Mama and Bessie's sister, Ma's oldest daughter and my Aunt Nellie. Aunt Nellie was the loveliest look-ing of Ma's girls, high cheekbones, fair skin and eyes as dark as the lake on a stormy day. Everyone said I was the image of Nellie, but in my opinion the lot of them were blind. All I saw in my dresser mirror was a mass of wild curly auburn colored hair at the top of a broomstick body. I soon found out though, that compared with Willie, I was plenty well off.

You'd think parents like Thomas and Nellie would have produced an award-winning baby. The sad truth is that Willie was born paralyzed on one side and hadn't been expected to live more than a few weeks. Mama told me how Ma had tried to console Nellie. "You view the back of the tapestry now, a threaded puzzle, but one day, you will turn it over and God's beautiful picture on the other side will reveal itself."

Upstairs in their bedroom Bessie whispered to her sister Barbara, "Those adages of Ma's don't explain a thing to poor Nellie."

"That's right," Mama agreed. "Nellie listens only to the cries of her baby in the hospital."

Willie lived, and after weeks of infant therapy, ended up with one arm he couldn't straighten out. He was also somewhat retarded. As though that weren't enough trouble for one child, his mother Nellie died suddenly of pleurisy, the same as Aunt Annie, Jeanette's mother, had, when Willie was eight years old. Six months after Nellie's death, during the summer of the raspberries, Willie's father Thomas handed the boy over to Grandma Bridget, who was Willie's grandma as well as mine, explaining that he'd found a new job two hundred miles east of Marquette in Sault Saint Marie.

That evening, Mama and Bessie rehashed this family news in Mama's and my bedroom. "Poor Willie," Bessie said while undoing the reddish brown braid at her back and shaking her hair loose. "I don't think his father ever loved him."

Mama's frown seconded Bessie's conclusion as she pulled her nightgown over her head. "He may get used to Willie's lame arm over time, but might never accept the boy's being retarded." Mama sat down at the edge of the bed. "Nellie loved him no matter," she said, voice quivering. "And would have kept on loving him."

Willie, two years older than me, was already big for nine when he settled into an upstairs bedroom with Uncle Danny and two or three boarders. In September, Mama enrolled Willie in second grade with me. During exercise class on his first day, our teacher, Miss Delany, asked us to do some bending and stretching exercises. "Reach your arms toward the ceiling as high as you can," she said.

Willie stood motionless while glaring down at his feet until Miss Delany noticed him. "William, you'll have to stay after school if you don't follow my instructions," she told him.

I figured Willie was too proud to explain that he couldn't move his arm, so I piped up for him. "That's not fair," I said. "Willie can't help it. He can't do the exercise. He was born that way. One arm is paralyzed."

Miss Delany turned bright pink, neck to forehead. "Oh, I'm so sorry, Willie," she said. "I didn't know. You can be excused from the stretching whenever you like."

I thought Willie might want to thank me when he rushed out of school ahead of me that afternoon, but instead he grabbed me with his good arm and shoved me behind a bush in the play yard. He whacked me hard across my face. "That'll teach you to shut your mouth about me in front of the class!" Then he gave me another smack on the other side of my head that knocked me to the ground. Before stomping away he sneered at me, blue eyes large, blond hair snarled and uncombed as usual, shirttail escaping his pants.

I clutched at my chest struggling for a breath while trying to console myself. At least from now on, I would know what to expect from Willie, and I'd have sense enough to duck.

I got to witness Willie's temper often but he kept that side of himself under raps at Ma's house. Whenever he got quiet or sullen at home, people simply declared he had good reason. And that was true enough. For one thing, his father never came to visit him. Mama told me, "Ruthie, you needn't envy those expensive gifts Willie's papa sends him. He buys them to salve his conscience for leaving his boy behind." She patted me on the head to make me feel better, but by then I was already picturing Willie's presents, a magic lantern, beautiful Teddy Roosevelt Safari game, store-bought clothes, and the brand new red bicycle that had just arrived.

"I believe his papa is a rat, Mama, but I can't stop dreaming about riding, no hands, down Genesee Street hill on that splendid bicycle."

Mama shook her head at me. "You never had a bike. You don't even know how to ride a bike, Ruthie."

I smiled and wiped my hands on my skirt; I was itching to steal that cycle. Looking at it made me feel like I had a nasty mosquito bite on my rear that I couldn't reach to scratch.

One afternoon I came home from school and Willie was nowhere in sight, yet his fire red bike leaned against the house out back as usual. Sashaying nonchalantly into the kitchen, I asked. "So where's Willie off to, Ma?"

She swished her heated iron across the sleeve of Da's shirt. "He's over at his friend Harold's house for an hour."

Blood rushing to my brain, stomach turning hoops and body on fire, I swung open the screen door, leaped from the top porch step to the grass and flew toward the crimson jewel. That cycle might have been the devil himself beckoning, teasing me, but I didn't give a hoot in hell. My right hand clasped the handlebars, the left hand the seat, and, before I could inhale, I was peddling around the house, then down our street.

Fast, faster, faster yet, driving like a drunken ore boat sailor, I kept going. Then, without warning, the bike and I lit out in different directions. I landed in the grass at the side of the road. The bike, still traveling like it had secret plans of its own, flopping to one side, then the other, shimmied finally to a stop, and then flipped over onto a mound of freshly hoed dirt.

I struggled up. Paying no mind to the scrapes on my legs, I dashed ahead to the bike. Seeing no glaring injuries to the flaming red surface, I crossed myself and said, "Thank you, God. I'll repay you for this. Whatever you want, it's yours."

While dragging the cycle back down the street to our yard, I made a plan: I'd set the bike against the house exactly where it was and give it a quick brushing off with the handkerchief in my pocket. Then I'd take every other step upstairs to my room, shut the door and pretend I'd been there all along.

If it hadn't been for Willie's undependability, not sticking to his original plan of being away an hour, my plan would have been brilliant. As I entered the yard, though, Willie smacked open the screen door with his good fist, and warm pee started to dribble down inside my long underwear into my shoes. Then Willie's good arm lurched toward me. I got the side of his elbow above my right ear, and he'd have gotten the other ear, too, if he'd had two arms, but he used his only good one to yank the bike handles from my hands. I tore into the house, up the back stairs and listened at the top step. I heard the back door slam and Willie go into the kitchen. Afraid to take a breath, I waited for him to snitch on me. But Willie didn't say a word to Ma about me stealing his bike.

I shot down the hall to my room, flipped the inside lock, fell onto my bed and tried to figure out what Willie was up to. Then it came to me. Willie had decided to handle differences between him and me on his own, never giving me permission to use his possessions, but if he caught me with a finger on one of them, he would mete out his own punishment.

He had me in a bind. I could take my beating from Willie or tell Ma he was smacking me around, have Ma ask why, and then get smacked a second time by Ma for whatever I'd done to rile up Willie.

You would think knowing my fate would have cured me. I honestly tried to keep my hands off Willie's presents for a while, but the temptation got too great. Besides, sometimes riding that bike and showing Willie I wasn't afraid of him seemed worth the price of ending up with a few bruises.

Well, that's how the war between Willie and me began, even before he and Ma became allies against me.

CHAPTER 5

Poor Willie

WHATEVER MY PERSONAL feelings toward Willie, I couldn't help but notice that life was a lot harder for him than for most people. He spent two years in grade two while I finished third grade, left my first schoolhouse and moved on to fourth grade at Alcott School a few blocks away on the corner of Fourth and Fisher. Concerned that Willie, now nearly ten, was not going to be promoted to third grade in the old school house, Ma convinced the parents of another problem pupil to pay half the tutoring fee for Willie and their daughter at the Northern State Normal School. This worked out well for me, because the girl's father, afraid that the two of them would get lost on their own, paid me a nickel to walk them to and from the state college in North Marquette twice a week.

Though I was seven, two years younger than they were, I brought them back and forth to the college for a whole year.

The tutoring, however, didn't help either of them much. The following September, Willie and the girl were both assigned to the "slow learners" group rather than third grade, and I lost my five-cent a week job.

Willie's "slow learner" class met upstairs in my old schoolhouse. Three rooms of the school held the first three grades; the fourth room was reserved for Skinny Richards, a six-foot tall, 140 pound truant officer and his conglomerate of incorrigible kids and slow thinkers. Skinny didn't pretend to teach anything to these kids; his job was to keep them off the streets. He invented his personal system of discipline that consisted of throwing at least one misbehaving kid down the stairs every week. Once he made the mistake of throwing a Chippewa Indian kid down the steps head first. The boy's two older brothers blasted into the school that afternoon, lifted Skinny up by the collar, dragged him outside, and cleaned his clock. The two brothers ended up in jail and Skinny ended up in the hospital.

A few years after that, conditions for the "slow thinkers" in the fourth room improved slightly. Chuck Olsen, a young, athletic male teacher who replaced Skinny, actually gave the kids a sampling of special tutoring just in case a few of them might qualify for the Manual Training Center at Marquette's high school. Unfortunately, these changes came too late for Willie, who had just finished his two years in Skinny's slow thinker class.

Ma certainly didn't give up on Willie, who was twelve by the end of his first year among the "the slow learners". She hired Miss Denton, the real third grade teacher, to tutor him all summer. This was the same Miss Denton who ended up teaching school until she was ninety-one. As soon as she retired, she took to wandering around town with a canvas bag over her shoulder and picking up string, nothing else, just string, that she found on the street. Nobody bothered her because she had helped so many of the town's adults as children and their children too. As respected as Miss Denton was, even she had little success with Willie. Ma, however, remained philosophical, mumbling for the hundredth time: "Who said it would be easy to make a silk purse out of a sow's ear?"

Miss Denton wasn't the end of Ma's efforts to educate Willie either. Ma never stopped trying to make it up to him for what he was missing. Too bad for me that her efforts were often at my expense, or so it seemed. There was an Episcopal chapel in South Marquette about two blocks from our house called Saint Margaret's Mission. This wasn't my church, but I stopped in there one day, and the nun in charge invited me to join their girls' club. "The Girls Friendly," as we fifth graders called ourselves, met in the chapel every Friday afternoon after school. As our winter project, we cut and sewed rags and rolled them into balls. In the spring we sold them all to a traveling rag carpet weaver to make money for the mission. As a reward, the youth leader promised that as soon as the weather turned warm enough he would take us on a combination picnic and overnight fishing trip near Big Bay.

I talked about the trip incessantly for weeks beforehand until one night my old enemy Squinty Eyes exploded. "Close your trap about that damn trip, will you girl!" he screeched, but everyone at the supper table glared at him and I jabbered on.

Frankie Moore, a big clumsy man who had frightened me by his size when he first came to live with us three years earlier, was now my favorite boarder. The day before my picnic and fishing trip Frankie asked me to follow him out to the back porch and sit next to him on a step. "We're going to whittle you a fishing pole from this old tree branch that'll be the envy of all parties at Saint Margaret's Mission."

He hadn't lied to me. When we finished I had in my hands the sleekest fish pole I'd ever been privileged to cast my eyes upon. "We should hang it in an art museum, Frankie," I said. His old puffy face blushed.

"Wait a minute." He lifted his huge body from the step and lumbered into the house. A few minutes later he returned. "Take these. They're my best hooks. Got them from a gypsy lady who gave them a good luck kiss."

I almost said I couldn't accept his special personal hooks, but they shone silvery and lovely in the sunlight and I said, "Wow, thank you," and slipped them into my jacket pocket. Then he took me out to the garden area and showed me how to dig up the best worms, leaving me alone and coming out to check on me every half hour or so to see how I was progressing.

Early Saturday morning I packed my gear in an old potato sack and was ready an hour early. Too excited to eat breakfast, I ran to the kitchen to kiss Mama goodbye. Ma who was at the tubs washing a colander of green beans under the faucet, suddenly whirled around. "Where does that girl think she's going, Barbara?" she was using her sharpest tongue, the one that made my arms cross and squeeze me tight across my middle.

Ma couldn't pretend she didn't know where I was going. Everybody knew; even Charlie and Gracie in their barn stalls knew. Mama clamored to my defense, telling Ma all over again about the trip. "This is the outing she's been looking forward to all winter." Mama's cheeks turned beet red.

Ma turned swiftly back to her colander of beans. "Ruthie can't go. It's Saturday. Churning day."

"Willie can do the churning this once," Mama said, not surrendering as usual, but with a pleading voice that was the same as waving a white flag in Ma's face. I wanted yell at her: "Mama, don't beg!"

"No, he can't," Ma said with finality, throwing out her "discussions over" chin. "Aunt Hattie asked Willie to come over to play checkers with Clayton this afternoon."

"Please God," I prayed, "Come up with a last minute miracle so Mama will have the courage to tell Ma to stick her head in the churner and leave it there." But it was over and I knew it. Ma nodded her head in my direction and then toward the barrel. I couldn't look at Mama. I just walked over and sat down in the chair next to the barrel. I wasn't about to satisfy my grandma with tears. Or else, maybe I was too full of hatred to cry.

Hours later when I finished the churning, Mama dressed me up in a fresh cotton dress and gave me twenty cents to go to the matinee at the Delft movie house. She grabbed me and hugged me at the front door before I left, and I saw that her eyes were swollen and red and I knew that she was the one who had been able to cry.

I slid into my seat in the back row of our theatre that was about the size of two parlors. I didn't care that the movie was stupid, a woman getting herself kidnapped by a mouse of a man she could have done in with one good belt to his chin. If I'd been with my friend Teresa we'd have been laughing our heads off, but Teresa was out at Big Bay that minute baiting her fish line at the side of a lovely wooded stream.

Since the matinee cost a nickel, I stopped at the Candy Kitchen for a chocolate sundae afterward and bought a nickel's worth of love candy taffy with my last nickel. I appreciated Mama wanting to make me feel better, but nobody could do that: I couldn't stop picturing my beautiful fishing pole and silvery hooks and fat worms going to waste in a sack on our back porch.

CHAPTER 6

Spitting into the Wind

MA'S FAVORITISMS OF Willie—serving him supper before me, not asking him to do housework or laundry or empty slop jars, and plenty else—upset me more every week. To calm down, I counted the ways I was more fortunate than Willie. Number one, I had a lot more friends than he did. And two, school had always been smooth sledding for me. This didn't help much though because Willie's defects weren't the only reason he got better treatment than I did from Ma. A bigger reason was his having been born a boy. And that really steamed me.

Willie himself flaunted his so-called superiority. Whenever I started to say something halfway smart, he interrupted. "You're only a girl. Who wants to hear what you say?"

He sauntered into the kitchen at noontime every day, sat at the table and ordered me to fix him lunch. The first time this happened a few months earlier I stuck out my tongue out at him. "Make your own rotten sandwich," I told him, unfortunately just as Ma happened to appear at the back door.

She stomped over to me and slapped me hard across the cheek and shrieked, "Make his lunch! And make it quick."

Willie let out a big guffaw, but as soon as Ma turned away, I sent him a message with my middle finger the way Willie's ruffian friends did to each other.

I'm the one who helped Ma every day, not Willie, and yet useless Willie was the one sitting at the kitchen table every day after that waiting for me to serve him. If I had had a shaker of arsenic, I'd have sprinkled a layer on his sandwich and happily watched him choke to death.

In December Ma assigned me to help her with her wool carding, a job I detested worse than emptying slop jars, but there was no escape. Ma was getting ready for her winter quilting bees. Every year she bought several bags of raw wool from nearby sheep farmers and carded the wool herself to save money. Setting up a workspace in the kitchen, she ordered any female unfortunate enough to meander into the room to sit down and card.

One particular night, I'd been at it for hours, taking handfuls of the filthy raw wool from a canvas bag, working the mess back and forth between two screen carders and letting the residue of seedy muck fall onto a newspaper spread across my lap. When the remaining wool became white and fluffy, I set it aside, reached into the bag and started all over again.

Since Ma had gone off to visit one of her cronies in the neighborhood after supper, I figured I'd be stuck carding till she came home. But then, unexpectedly, Mama showed up in the kitchen. "Mama, can I go sleigh riding for a little while, please?" I begged. "I've been carding ever since supper." Only then did I notice that Mama had washed her long dark hair and let it cascade over her shoulders. She had also changed into her wool suit, dark blue fitted jacket and ankle length skirt. "Where you going, Mama?" I asked her.

"This is my night to go to Ladies' Club meeting." She nodded toward the wash tubs. "All right, you can go sleigh riding if you dry the rest of the supper dishes."

"Will I?" I bounced out of the chair and over to the sink. I was happy to be set loose to go outside and just as happy to see Mama dressed up lovely. By the looks of Mama in fact, I suspected she and Aunt Bessie had more planned for the evening than their Ladies' Club meeting. I stole another look at my pretty young mama. "Have a good time after your meeting, too," I said.

I knew I was being too fresh for my own good, but Mama glanced back at me and smiled. "You're getting to be a smarty pants, aren't you, girl?"

When I returned from sleigh riding at eight-thirty, I slipped quietly through the back door and then spotted Ma in the kitchen, back at her wool carding. My heart sank. "Where have you been till this hour?" she cried out to me.

Gazing down at my snow boots, I mumbled, "Sleigh riding, Ma."

"And who gave you permission to go?"

"My mother did." I stared straight at her this time because Mama's authority was being questioned again, for the thousandth time.

"I see," said Ma. "I guess you'll have to make up for time lost by doing more carding now, then."

"I'm so sleepy. Can I please go to bed, Ma? I'll card tomorrow. I'll come straight home from school. Honest."

"I should say not." Pushing herself away from the carding bench, Ma stood. "I'll tell you when you can go to bed. Sit down here."

My eyelids closing and jerking open, head falling onto my chest and startling me awake again, I kept shoving my fingers through the muck. Nearly falling out of my chair once, I grabbed the table just in time. At ten-thirty, Willie burst through the back door letting a gust of cold wind in with him and Ma scurried out of her sitting room and back down the hall to greet him. Breaking out in a delighted smile, she asked, "Did you have a nice time with your friends, Willie? I hope you remembered to be careful. It can be icy and treacherous on the streets this time of night."

Sighing with relief, I got up from my chair and took a few steps toward the stairwell to follow Willie upstairs, but Ma's voice blasted out from behind me: "Where do you think you're going? You're not finished yet." With that, she whisked herself around and marched back to her room.

I heard her door close and the inside lock snap, and I knew I would be working until Mama got home. I guessed this was Mama's punishment for giving me permission to do something.

Mama opened the front door about eleven o'clock, and, seeing the light at the end of the hall, hurried out to the kitchen. Horrified to see my head resting on my chest and my fingers struggling with the filthy wool, she whispered, "Come to bed, Ruthie." With her arm at my waist, she helped me out of the chair and up the back stairs. In our bedroom we got into our nightgowns; Mama crawled into bed next to me and held me close to her the rest of the night.

At breakfast I ate my bread and butter and drank my glass of milk without speaking. I wished Mama would tell Ma we were moving out that day, but this time I felt sorry for Mama instead of impatient for a change. The wool carding incident made me see more clearly the way things were for Mama and me. The truth is, Mama and I had nowhere else to go. We were stuck together like two captives in the castle of a cruel queen mother. I wanted to call Ma every four letter word name I wasn't supposed to know, and to kick Willie hard right where you were never supposed to kick boys. I had to sit on my hands to keep them from knocking everything off the table to the floor.

❧

In spite of Ma's claim on me, I tried to treat Mama like a real mama after that, completing the smallest chore for her with great fanfare: "Don't

bother me now, I'm busy doing a job for my mama,"
I repeated like a Hail Mary at least twice a day.

Mama for her part almost never punished me,
that is, until the day Ol' Lady O'Brien, the neighborhood snoop, saw me leaving the lumberyard a
block away from home. I loved leaping off six or
seven feet high piles of two by fours with the nine
and ten year old boys who congregated at the sawmill after school. Mama, insisting this was dangerous play, had ordered me not to go there, but I
couldn't seem to resist the temptation.

I thought Mrs. O'Neil might land on her arse,
the way she whipped down to our house to squeal
on me to Mama. Mama, still in her apron, left Mrs.
Busybody in our kitchen and she raced up the
street after me. Grabbing me by my coat collar,
she hauled me down the block to our house. "You
don't want to grow to adulthood? Is that right,
young lady? One day you'll get yourself killed rough
housing with those toughs."

We reached our back porch and Mama yelped
at me with a stranger's pitched angry voice. "Be a
tomboy if you have to, but do it without giving me
heart failure!" Then she stood there looking baffled as to what to do next. I was embarrassed for
her because she'd never slapped me. I wanted to
point to my rear end and say, "Here's where you
do it, Mama." Instead, she threw her head back
and shouted, "Get up to your room and stay there.
There'll be no supper for you tonight."

I hated staying in my room alone with nothing to do. An hour later, I was wishing Mama had
wholloped me and got done with it, but I was

proud of Mama's firmness either way. I was staring numbly out the window when my bedroom door flew open and there was Ma, of all people, carrying a tray. "Here's a nice butter sandwich and a helping of cabbage salad for you," she said. "You must be hungry."

"Thank you," I said, but she was already gone from the room and padding down the hall. I gobbled up the supper in a hurry, but minutes later the food sat in my stomach like I'd swallowed a block of quarry granite.

I got into bed and closed my eyes, but they kept popping right open. The harder I tried to fall asleep, the more awake I became. Finally, I got out of bed and crept over to the window, not to pray exactly, but to find the moon and think. Why had I gone against Mama's wishes by eating the supper from Ma? Sure, partly I was hungry. But ever since Ma left my room, I'd been picturing Ma and me in the country again, Ma with her arm around my shoulder letting me slide closer to her, the noontime sun warming us. Earlier, when she had set her tray on my lap, I had wished for a split second that she would stroke my hair and say something nice. I guess I would have burrowed my head into her neck and snuggled up to her. Maybe that's the real reason I was feeling disloyal to Mama.

I pulled back the curtain in search of the Milky Way. Seeing the clusters of beautiful stars made me wonder if God believed Grandma Bridget was a saint like everyone claimed she was.

Backing away from the window, I tiptoed down the hall to the back stairs and sat on the top step. I listened to nighttime noises coming from the kitchen, the grinder's grrrrrrr preparing coffee for tomorrow's breakfast, wood crunching against wood, Willie filling the wood box near the stove, the scraping of a knife, Grampa William, my Da, whittling shavings and laying the fire for morning, the back door opening and closing, Willie heading to the woodbin for more logs, steam hissing on the stove, the teapot heating water for Da's and Ma's nightly hot toddy.

I wanted to scramble down the stairs and crawl into Da's lap, but Ma wouldn't have any of that. I'd have been daft not to grasp that I wasn't the grand-daughter Ma wanted. Was it too late to transform myself into *that* girl, the one who answered, "Yes, Ma" with a smile to every request? If I bowed to Ma's will as Mama and Uncle Danny and Bessie and Da and the rest of the family did, would Ma love me as much as she loved Willie? Maybe she would I guessed.

Exhausted from too much supposing for a nine year old, I lifted my bottom from the step and shuffled back to my room. Then, to my surprise, as I got into bed and huddled under my quilt, an inspiration, like a falling star from the universe of truth, drifted into my brain: *I could never give Ma what she wanted.* I'd rather spit into the wind every single day of the year than turn myself into the timid little imbecile Ma wanted just for a few of her lousy hugs. And that was a fact I'd have to live with.

CHAPTER 7

The Hogans

MA HATED IDLENESS, and I guess this applied to pianos as well as people. She had an old-fashioned piano, curlicue fancy trimming all around the top and sides, sitting in her parlor doing nothing. Her three older daughters used to play Irish ballads and classical music on it, but they had all married and left home. So as soon as I turned nine, she ordered Mama to sign me up for piano lessons from Professor Magnum at his home on Baraga Avenue.

On the day of our first blizzard that fall, I headed over to Professor Magnum's home clutching five dollars in a small Indian leather purse to pay for the four lessons I'd had so far. I was amazed that Mama could spare a dollar a week from her pittance of a salary from Ma. Maybe Mama hoped I would have some sort of talent in my genes from the Hogan side, but I could have told her she was wasting her money.

The weather was getting stormier by the minute with high winds and snow swirling around me. With one hand to my throat holding my coat closed, I grasped my music exercise roll under my arm and hung onto my Indian purse with the other hand. At the corner of Front Street and Baraga, where the wind whips up over the hill from the lake, a gust suddenly hit me in the face, blowing my purse clear out of my hand. I chased after it toward the lake but quickly lost sight of it. My hands and feet almost frozen numb, I searched for the purse nearly all the way down to the harbor and back with my heart hammering in my ears. How was I ever going to face Mama or Ma?

I was crying my eyes out when I reached Front Street again and saw Vangie Pellissier waving to me from the window of her news shack. I spun around and between gusts of snow, saw her motioning for me to come inside. The door swung open, and Vangie wrapped her big comforting arms around me. "Get in here. You're freezing," she said pulling me in by my coat collar and slamming the door shut. She raised her eyebrows and smiled slyly. "And besides, there's someone I want you to say hello to."

Glancing around the news and tobacco, past stacks of newspapers and magazines on shelves, I recognized everyone, Mr. Sweeney, the fish market owner, and a Merchant Marine off one of the iron boats and Mr. Swenson from the city library reading a newspaper—but one person, a shabbily dressed man, unshaven with straggly hair hugging the collar of his worn coat.

"There's your father," Vangie said, pointing to the same man now warming himself by the pot-bellied stove.

Why was Vangie telling me such a lie? I backed up, wishing I were still out in the blizzard. I was supposed to believe that old tramp was my father? I waited for everyone to laugh at her joke and nobody did. This person was nothing like the papa who came to rescue Mama and me in my dreams. That papa was handsome and rich and dressed in a black coat with a fur collar. But then, what did I know? I hadn't seen my papa since I was three and that was six years ago.

"Go say hello," Vangie said nudging me toward this stranger.

"That's not fair, Vangie," said the man. "I'd frighten the devil himself today." He flicked some old cigar ashes from his lap and wiped off his hands on his coat sleeves. Lowering his head, he studied the floor. Seemed to me he'd rather be somewhere else – the same as me.

I felt like I might be good and sick before I reached him. Brushing the remainder of tears from my cheeks, I made myself look at the dark, uncombed beard and then, down at the ragged coat. When I got closer, he touched my hand and I was surprised at how warm his skin felt on my freezing cold fingers.

"What's the matter, girl?" he asked, blue eyes dimming everything else about him, beard, untrimmed hair, and even the tattered clothing.

I remembered how Mama had described Papa's eyes to Bessie late one night when they thought I was asleep. "Blue as an August sky," she had said. Maybe, then, this was my papa. Suddenly, for no reason at all, I started to bawl all over again, and, before I knew it, I was telling him the whole story about my purse and the storm and the money. When I finished, another bucket of tears gushed from my eyes and slobbered down my cheeks.

Like a magician, this stranger whisked a clean white hankie from his torn pocket and set it in my hand. While I blew my nose, he called out to Vangie. "Call Barb, will you, Vangie? Explain to her about the purse and the fierce weather. Ask her not to be too hard on Ruthie."

He turned back to me and smiled for the first time. "Sorry you had to view your Papa like this. I wanted to clean up before seeing you."

"Were you going to come to see me?" I didn't mean to put him on the spot, but I had a right to know, didn't I?

"Is that what you think? That your Papa would come all the way home to Marquette and not see you?"

"I couldn't make a guess about that after six years, sir," I said looking straight at him.

"Ah . . . Hmm. Has it been that long? Really? Well, it's not like I haven't thought about you every day." He wrung his hands together and stared at me for several seconds. "Sorry I'm not the papa you would have wanted," he said.

"You'd have been better than none," I told him. I didn't mean to sound fresh or mean. I was only trying to be honest.

"Not sure if that's true, Ruthie." He got up from his stool in front of the stove. "Still, I'm glad you're not afraid to speak your mind." At least, I was relieved to see that he was as tall as I had daydreamed him. "Next time we meet I'll be so scrubbed up you'll probably take me for Prince Charming." He bent down and fastened the button at the collar of my coat. "You going to get home all right?"

"Oh, sure," I answered as he walked me to the door. Outside, I shoved the hankie deep down into my front pocket and pushed myself against sheets of snow down the Front Street hill. If the hankie was still there tomorrow I would figure today had actually happened.

By the time I reached home, Grandma Bridget had repeated her phone conversation with Vangie Pellisher to Mama . I watched as Mama shook her shoulders and frowned. "If Dominic was so concerned, why didn't he give her the five dollars?" Then she gazed down at her shoes for a second, an exhausted sigh escaping her lips. "Oh, I'm sure he didn't have the five dollars. He would have given it to her if he'd had it."

"I wouldn't be sure about that, Barbara," Ma commented and I had a hard time holding onto my foot that was itching to kick her in the shin.

That night I said a prayer asking God to keep Papa from feeling too bad about not having the five dollars. The next morning, as though answering my prayer, Aunt Nellie, one of my father's sisters, called Mama to say she and her husband Nook wanted me to come by after school "since Dommy will only be in town a few days and he wants to have another visit with Ruthie."

"Please, please, let me go," I begged my mother. Mama got a tongue lashing later from Ma for saying yes, but still Mama kissed me before I left for school that morning. "Have a good time, Ruthie," she whispered.

I could hardly sit still in class all day counting the minutes till again I'd see my papa and any of the Hogans who would be there. I loved visiting the Hogan house on Fisher Street every chance I got, for birthdays, to pick up a Christmas present or just for tea with Aunt Nellie. The Hogans didn't have much else, but they sure knew how to have a good time.

As usual, everybody made a fuss when I walked into the house. "Oh, Ruthie. Pretty as ever," Aunt Nellie squealed, taking me by the hand into the parlor.

Even though I was nine, my father lifted me into his lap and kept me there most of the afternoon. I didn't twitch a muscle for fear he would think I wanted him to put me down. All washed and clean, beard and hair trimmed, wearing a starched white shirt and smelling like lavender, he didn't look a bit like the bum from the day before. Bet a lot of ladies could have mistaken him for Prince Charming. And I'm the one he'd chosen for the afternoon, asking me questions about school and friends and baseball. He blushed when he mentioned Mama but I pretended not to notice as I informed him, "She gets more beautiful every day. Everybody says so. The male boarders get downright fainty when she enters the room."

Aunt Nellie played the piano, my father sang and three cousins danced the fling. Just about all the Hogans were there except the traitor, Uncle Eddie, all alone in his mansion in Minneapolis. Even Ambrose, my father's youngest brother, had arrived home that day. He'd been traveling with a New York Vaudeville Troup for a couple of years and caught a train from Milwaukee just to see Dommy. What a show Ambrose gave us, one I'd never forget, Irish jigs, lip music and piano. By the time Ambrose finished, I knew I must be the only Hogan alive with no talent whatsoever. So what was the good of being a Hogan without any talent? How I'd loved to have dazzled them with a brilliant song or a dance.

Right in the middle of one of Ambrose's ballads, my father set a hand under my chin and turning my head to the side, seemed to be examining me. Was he criticizing me? I could hardly breath waiting for him to speak. "Hmm. You had blue eyes like me and blond hair when you were very little," he said. "I see your eyes have turned brown now, haven't they? And your hair is getting dark like your mother's."

Well, that did it. I figured I was a monumental disappointment to him in about every way there was. My throat tightened up. I was afraid the tears would start again and he'd think me a first class crybaby. But just then Danny, another of my father's brothers, dropped in and everyone went berserk: "Oh, Danny, oh Danny! Get yourself in here."

Danny, the police officer and pride of the family, had recently been promoted to Marquette Police Chief. Because of his small frame he couldn't arrest anyone without knocking him out first, yet he was so adored in town that nobody complained. And, that afternoon, he became my personal hero as well. He sent my spirits spiraling upward with every note out of his mouth while offering a rendition of "Galway Bay" that made the dog run for the door. Nevertheless, everyone applauded the same as they had for Ambrose. My heart nearly burst open with joy and pride, that I could, after all, it seemed, be one of the rowdy, no-good Hogans and Dominic's daughter even with a voice that sounded like a rooster crowing on a fence post.

CHAPTER 8

The Quilting Bee Secrets

WHEN MAMA AND I were finally alone in the kitchen that evening before supper she asked me for details about my afternoon at the Hogans. When I finished my report, talking more to herself than to me, it seemed, she said, "I had wonderful times in that house before your dad and I were married," She dropped the last potato into a pot of boiling water, the steam pasting frizzy curls to her forehead. She brushed them away with the back of her arm, eyes watering too now and asked, "And how did your papa look today, Ruthie?"

"Handsome, Mama," I told her. "Hair and beard clipped, lovely stiff shirt." I dried the last of the silverware in the dish drain for supper. "You didn't tell me his voice is as soft as Da's and that his laugh is so hearty." I picked up the rest of the clean silver to bring to the dining table. "I understand why you fell in love with him, Mama."

"Thank you. That'll be our secret, Ruthie."

Ma bustled into the dining room a while later with a bowl of turnips, set them on the table and clanked a fork to the side of Da's water glass. "Attention, everybody." She waited for silence before making an announcement to all family members and boarders. "I need volunteers to ready the parlor for my quilting bee. Tomorrow is our first weekly bee." With the wool carding finished, I could see that Ma had turned her energies toward preparing for her winter bees. The parlor, used only for wakes and special visitors the rest of the year, would have to be emptied of everything except the piano and settee to make room for the quilt stretcher frames.

"How many hands do I see?" she inquired. Fifteen hands rose in unison, surely no one at the table believing they had a choice in the matter. Then Ma rapped Da's glass a second time. "And don't forget, the parlor will be off limits to one and all for six weeks while the bees are in session. Same as always."

A week later, on the evening of the first bee, as soon as Ma's three neighborhood cronies had arrived about seven o'clock, I pinned my fanny to the top step of the front staircase to eavesdrop. I'd never paid attention to Ma's bees other years, but I had been feeling restless ever since my exciting day at the Hogans'.

Sipping their coffee and biting into fresh hot donuts from one of their kitchens, they chatted as they worked, mostly reminiscing, but sharing town gossip as well. To me, the conversation always seemed to be going nowhere, tacking sideways and back and forth. But then, surprisingly, there it would be back on course. "But, for the grace of God," said plump, pleasant Molly Smyth, Ma's oldest friend on earth. "Last summer's tornado could have wiped out the town instead of just sheering off a dozen rooftops."

"That was bad enough," Ma said. "You see the rosy side of everything, Molly."

"Remember that three legged potato sack race every year at the St. Peter's Church picnic, Bridget?" Molly asked changing the subject. "The other night I dreamed about the race I won when I was twelve.. Of all the crazy things."

I could tell they were off and running, one by one, going to relate tales from the last century. If they were going to tell stories that old, I figured I'd go back to my room. But that very moment, Liddy said, "Too bad your childhood got cut short, Bridget," and I set my rear down again. Liddy had always been my favorite crony. She wasn't a stubborn Mick with set opinions like Ma. Secretly, in fact, I'd wished many times that I'd got her for a grandma instead of Ma, but that was a wasted wish, wasn't it?

Nipping at Libby's bait, Ma answered, "You mean when my father made me quit school after only one year?" Ma sounded strange all of a sudden, so weak I had to strain to hear her. "I hadn't even learned to read by then," Ma said. "I don't blame my father, mind you. Who else was going to take care of all the babies in our house while my mama was out tending to other people's homes?"

"Wasn't I lucky to get five years of schooling?" Molly reminded them.

"That's because you weren't the oldest girl," Liddy said. "Bridget wasn't that fortunate."

I was stunned by the news that Ma had had only one year of schooling; I had always believed Grandma Bridget knew everything that was worth knowing. For sure, she wasn't dumb. Smart enough to keep us all alive, wasn't she? She had opinions about everything, the town, the church, the country and the rest of the world too. Da read the newspaper out loud to her every evening; I had supposed that husbands liked to do that. This startling information was starting to sink in: *Could it be possible that Ma couldn't read?* That she couldn't read any of the hundreds and hundreds of books at the Marquette Public Library?

Using her frail voice again, Ma said, "My papa always told me I'd have to go to work as soon as I was tall enough. My bad luck was being tall enough when I was only ten." Ma forced a laugh at what must have been a very old joke.

Mary, the fourth member of the quartet, said, "If that had been me, I'd have made it to eighteen before being carted out of town." Mary reminded me of a delicate bird with her robin-red hair and voice sweet as a canary. But Mama told me not to be fooled by appearances, that Mary was actually a wise old owl.

"I earned two dollars a week taking care of our brood at home," Ma said. "Papa took one dollar to save and the priest took the other." She chuckled again in a way that made me want to cry.

"I really meant cutting your childhood short a few years later, Bridget," Liddy said. "When your papa sent you into the boonies to work at that awful Lumberjack Inn."

The room went silent for a whole minute at least, and then Mary asked, "Are you ever going to tell us your secret about the terrible thing that happened in the woods that night, Bridget?"

Something about that question shot me up out of my seat on the step and darting up the stairs to my room. What dreadful thing could have happened to Grandma Bridget in the woods near a place called the Lumberjack Inn? Dropping my dress on the floor, I pulled on my nightgown and dove into bed and shivered and yanked the bed quilt over my head. Maybe tomorrow I'd have the courage to ask Mama for the answer.

CHAPTER 9

The Mahaars

THE DAY AFTER eavesdropping on the quilting bee, I couldn't stop wondering what awful secret Grandma Bridget had kept to herself all these years. As the afternoon wore on my curiosity only grew. Ma's mother, my great-grandma Katie Mahaar, lived four blocks away from us but she was getting too old to be bothered with a lot of questions from me. And her husband Michael, my great-grandpa, had died a few years back, so I couldn't ask him anything, could I? Besides, what was I going to ask them if I could? "Why were you so mean to your oldest daughter Bridget, taking her out of school and sending her to frightful place called the Lumberjack Inn?" And how could Mama answer the same questions? On the way home from school I thought of one remote possibility to dig up my own information on the Mahaars. To do it, I'd have to be braver than I felt.

I'd have to talk myself into climbing a ladder in Uncle Danny's and Willie's bedroom and pushing open a hatch door at the top and crawling into a dark little attic cubbyhole all by myself. I wouldn't be such a coward if Willy hadn't threatened once a week to lock me up in there. But wouldn't it be worthwhile if I happened to find a clue or two leading to the discovery of Ma's secret?

The best time to sneak into Willie's room would be right after my chores were finished and before Willie got home around four o'clock and while there was still sunlight streaking though a foot by foot window facing the back yard. When the perfect moment arrived, I gulped in a big breath, tiptoed over to the ladder and set a foot on the bottom rung, then the next and the next. At the top I had to shove hard to open the hatch even a slit and immediately got hit in the face with a whiff of musty sickening smelling air. If I'd heard a haunted ghost noise—which, thank you, Baby Jesus, I didn't—I'd have scuttled down the ladder faster than rats from a sinking ship.

Once inside, I noted the curtains of cobwebs clinging to the walls and layers of dust covering six or seven boxes and three large steamer trunks. What did I think I'd locate here to help reveal Ma's secret? The best find would be a journal supposedly written by Katie Mahaar during her journey with her husband Michael from Ireland, then to Michigan. The problem is: Katie had sworn she'd given her journal to Ma for safekeeping and Ma had insisted many times that she didn't have it. Neither of them had ever bothered to prove the other one wrong, so about a year ago, after one of my eavesdropping sessions on the stairs, I decided there had never been a journal at all and both women were too stubborn to admit the truth. Now, of course, I was hoping I was wrong.

Whew! I nearly fainted from the odor of moldy clothes and dank smelling objects the second I wrenched open the first leather trunk. Pawing through this first trunk carefully, I fingered ancient baby clothes gently and untied ribbons cautiously from boxes of wedding and birthday mementos. Then I told myself to hurry, that I dare not use valuable time inspecting things now. I was searching for a particular item.

I rushed through the rest of the trunks with no luck finding the journal so I sat my bum down on a dilapidated box and rested a minute before starting in on the boxes. But then I noticed writing slightly smudged on a box directly in front of me and I leaped to my feet, bent over to inspect the handwriting more closely and read *Michael Mahaar Property* written in tiny feminine script.

I would have ripped the box apart if I had to, but no need; the cardboard fell open with barely a touch. My fingers went wild weaving under and over the contents, mostly old papers and brown photographs that I tossed aside and kept digging. At first I ignored an oblong object cradled among the papers figuring it to be another framed photograph. I had started to push it to one side when I decided to pull it out and give it a look.

I had to be dreaming. In my hand was a slim, leather bound notebook. I wanted to stay calm, but my fingers trembled as I opened the cover. On page one in the same delicate handwriting, I read: "Journal of Kathleen Mahaar—Ireland, June, 1851."

I stared at the treasure I'd been searching for, the journal that I'd only half believed existed.

Clutching at my great-grandmother's journal from sixty years ago, I perched myself on top of one of the leather steamer trunk and flipped through the pages quickly reading whatever happened to catch my eye:

May 10, 1847. "Crossing Atlantic Ocean to Canada is difficult in crowded ship. We sleep in berths stacked on top of each other in cheap passage area below deck.

August 14, 1847. Traveling across Canada to Niagara Falls, Ontario is tedious and long, but better than ship. At least I'm not seasick. Michael is a good-natured traveler. Better than me.

June 12, 1852. "First years in Canada have been hard. Our daughter Bridget was born June 13, 1852. We have barely enough money to feed ourselves or little Bridget and now another is on the way.

August 18, 1854. We are forced to pile our few possessions into a horse drawn wagon and cross the border into the United States at Niagara Falls tomorrow morning. Our third baby is due in four months. I hope jobs and pay are better in New York State.

July 18, 1856. "Odd jobs are more plentiful in New York State. But income is no better than in Canada. Too little to support three children and now a fourth on the way.

June, 5 1857. Fourth baby, third son born.

June 20, 1857. Today Michael got news of thriving and growing iron ore mining and shipping industry in theUpper Penninsula of northern Michigan. Michael has scraped up a few dollars for the trip. Day after tomorrow we pack up the wagon and start out for Michigan. Shortest route to northern Michigan is crossing back into Canada and heading west.

June 21, 1857. On second day of trip we have reached town of Hamilton. We have pulled into a wooded area outside city limits to sleep a few hours before Michael takes up the reins again tomorrow.

June 22, 1857. With three children rolled up in quilts and asleep in the wagon, I climbed up front to sit next to Michael and coddled the new baby in my lap under a shawl. I had a good warm feeling in me today as I spread a blanket across Michael's knees and buttoned my jacket to the neck to ward off early morning chill. It is summer, of course. Nobody would travel to the North Country in fall or winter. Even spring is uncertain. "Let the children sleep as long as possible," I told Michael. "They'll be hungry whether they wake up now or later." Now I'll pray again that the food will last til we can replenish it.

June 29, 1857. One week later. We passed back into the United States on the Michigan border at Port Huron on the southern tip of Lake Huron today.

July 10, 1857. We have traveled twelve more days north in Michigan to Mackinaw City. Arrived here with our two-year-old boy recovering from the croup, our three-year-old boy and four-year-old Bridget, both hungry, tired and irritable. Our baby, thank the Lord, is doing well. We purchased more canned milk, flour, sugar, potatoes, beans, dried fruit and coffee at a country store, enough to last through the remainder of the trip, we hope. Just outside of town I boiled potatoes and heated beans over our campfire. The children were happy to get out of the wagon and romp wildly through the surrounding tall grass.

July 11, 1857. Today, nudging and pulling our horse and pushing the overloaded wagon from behind, we boarded a ferryboat that took us across the Straights of Mackinaw to Saint Ignace on the Upper Peninsula of Michigan. The ride was lovely, sunny but cool.

From St. Ignace, we turned northwestward to cross the grasslands, rocky hills and thick forests. We are sharing the trail with deer, brown bear and all manner of small critters.

July 16, 1857. We found the rough lumber haul-
ing road we'd heard about that took us all the
way to Lake Superior. Ten hours later when
we caught our first glimpse of this immense
body of water, more an ocean than a lake, Michael halted the horse and wagon. 'Get out,
the lot of you to gaze at this clear blue water
and uninhabited shore.' he ordered lifting all
three children from the wagon and setting
them on the ground. I climbed out from the
front clutching the baby to my heart. Michael
reached his arm around my waist. I rested my
head against his shoulder. Suddenly Michael
howled to the heavens, it seemed: "Praise
God for bringing us safely to this glorious
place." We climbed back into the wagon and
followed the lake's coastline toward a host of
lights flickering in the distance.

July 17, 1857. We reached the Port of Marquette at 2:00 A.M. and parked in a field on
the town border. Lying on the bed mat together Michael brought me close to him and
kissed me and resting his head on my breast
started to cry. "I love you," he said. "I love
you." And we both fell into a heavy sleep.

July 18, 1857. This morning we headed toward
the south end of town where a livery stable
owner told us we'd find the cheapest rents.
We were shocked, but happy, to be greeted
by a colony of Irish settlers who had arrived
a few months earlier. By sundown, we had
rented a two-room tar paper house with

the few remaining coins in our moneybox. These Irish are as bad off as we are but they say they share supplies and help new-comers to find odd pieces of furniture and work.

November 20, 1862. In the five years we've been here, Marquette has become a lovely little town, houses built on the sides of hills, Lake Superior at its northern border, wooded forest forming boundaries to the south and west, farmland to the east. Michael can still get unskilled work on the docks and I get hired easily to clean homes of the wealthy lumber and mining families. But this is not what we do best. We are farmers, country people. But here in northern Michigan the farmland is rocky soil, difficult to till, in any case, owned by Swedes, Norwegians and Finns who settled here before us.

January 1, 1870. One thing I know. Even the hard labor Michael and I do would support us decently if there wasn't another infant born every year. Eight and Bridget isn't ten yet.

Suddenly realizing I'd lost track of time I closed the journal. I was going to be in trouble soon, if I wasn't already. Quickly, I repacked the Mahaar box stuffing the journal between papers at the bottom where I had found it. Luckily for me, I slipped out of Willie's room without running into him and got myself down to the kitchen to help before Ma missed me.

I kept my adventure in the attic to myself, but later in my room I thought a lot about what I'd read in Great Grandma Katie's journal. I tried to imagine all those people in an eight-foot by five-foot wagon for all those days. Four-year-old Bridget perhaps hushing two younger children, maybe changing the baby's diaper to let her mother sleep for a few hours. I pictured Michael and Katie, so young then, bumping along, saying rosaries under the stars and praying they'd all be alive when they reached Marquette. No wonder Ma called me a thankless child. Compared to her childhood, she must think I'm living the life of an English royal princess. As for Ma's one year of schooling, I didn't believe now that they meant to be cruel. In fact, I wondered now how they had spared their oldest daughter for that long. But, if they weren't to blame for Bridget's bad childhood, who was?

The priests told us that all children were gifts from God. If that's true I guess He could have given a few less gifts to the Mahaars. Out of nowhere, that very second, a thought trotted into my brain and galloped out my mouth: *God is to blame then!* I said. Just like that – outloud. At once, a giant drum started to beat in my ears and I shot up off my bed. I leaped across the floor and huddled in the corner of the room behind the rocker. Blaming God for something is surely the worst sin of all. A sin so bad a person could be struck dead for committing it, I'll bet.

Even with my body plastered to the wall and my insides playing leapfrog I couldn't seem to repent. In fact, in the meantime another blasphemous thought had settled in on me: *If God sent all those babies, why didn't he send enough food to feed them?*

CHAPTER 10

The Lumberjack Inn

I HAD QUIT spying on the biddies for a few weeks, but on the night of the last bee, their hoots of laughter aroused my curiosity again. Tossing *Oliver Twist* to my bed, I plunked down on the top step on the front staircase for a final listen. Da, instead, put on a clean shirt and escaped to the sanity of his friend Mr. Murphy's pub.

With snow melting on the roads and icicles dripping from the windows and most of the quilts designed, stuffed, sewn and stretched, one for each home and each daughter and daughter-in-law, the women had settled into an evening of raucous banter. Nobody, friends, family, townsfolk, not even clergy at St. Michaels Church, was safe from their tongues that evening. I had to plaster a hand to my mouth a few times to stop from giggling at conversation I shouldn't have been listening to in the first place. It wasn't their yarns that got me laughing though, it was the way they kept howling their heads off. Which is why I was caught off guard when suddenly the talk took a serious turn. Out of the blue, Grandma Bridget picked up on the mystery of the Lumberjack Inn that they'd left hanging weeks earlier.

"Molly, you remember the day Papa told me I would be going hours away to Grand Marais to work as a chambermaid in the Lumberjack Inn?"

"Like yesterday," Molly said. "You cried all day and night."

"And pleaded with him for days not to send me away." Ma's little girl voice had returned. "For years I asked myself why I didn't refuse to go. But, then one day, I realized there wasn't a bloody other thing I could have done differently at age twelve. Other than hide out in the woods with the deer and wildcats and black bear, maybe."

"And another thing, we didn't disobey our parents back then. The priest would have been hammering at our door the next day," Libby said.

"I felt like a dried out twig my last day at home, broken in two and tossed to the winds," Ma said. "Numb all over and saying goodbye to my mother and brothers and sisters and friends. I didn't speak a word to my father during the entire trip into the wooded country or after we arrived at the Lumberjack Hotel in Grand Marais."

Molly inserted, "I cried for weeks after you were gone," "I missed you so much."

"All I remember now about the hotel is the owner, that hefty, humorless man who worked all of the girls fifteen hours a day doing the laundry and cleaning, making beds, emptying slop pans. 'Big Swede,' they called him. Why he wanted everything sparkling clean for all those old drunken woodsmen, I don't know.

Ma sucked in a breath. "Oh, yes, I can't forget my wood plank cot with the lumpy mattress either. I used to wonder how many other Irish girls had slept on it before me. Six of us slept in a bit of a room with one two by two foot window too high to see out. Two years later when I turned fourteen, I prayed to the Lord that He would have something better in mind for each of us in that room than this. "Anything will be better than this, Lord," I whispered.

"Then halleluiah!" Ma yelped. The others gasped so I imagined Ma swinging her arms above her head. "I figured God had come through for us the next morning when we spied the notice on the hotel bulletin board advertising Saturday night dances at St. John's Church hall five miles away. Hiking to and from the dance and arriving back at the Lumberjack Inn at 6:00 A.M. in time to go to work on Sunday mornings was no trouble at all if it got us through the rest of the week."

"A girl might as well be cursed by the devil as be the oldest child," Libby repeated.

"Oh," Molly said, squelching a choke in her throat. "I was attending school at the same time you were living in that horrible place." She paused. "And then having that horrible thing happen in the woods."

"Are you ever going to tell us what happened that night, Bridget?" It was Mary asking.

The room went eerily silent for a full minute. Ma finally spoke. "You know what must have happened. What's the good of talking about it now?"

"Might help to air it with your oldest friends. Even now." Mary said, her gentle tone might have convinced the Pope to make a confession from St. Peters balcony, but I wasn't sure if it would affect Ma at all. In any case, good sense should have told me to turn tail and run. But I couldn't move a muscle.

"You don't have to tell us," Molly said. "Unless you want to."

I hugged my ribs tight with both arms. Was I at last going to hear the secret Ma had kept to herself this long?

"I wish I'd been able to forget," Ma said. "But I remember like it happened last night."

I was sure I heard four separate breaths taken in and held. Then Ma began in the tiny voice, words coming from a place far removed from our parlor:

"The other girls aren't with me; I'm alone, starting down the path for home. I have left the dance to get an early start back to the hotel. I see something move behind a tree. The size of a black bear, but not a bear. The figure comes out of the darkness. I see it is a young lumberjack I danced with earlier. He greets me in his own language, Norwegian I believe. As he comes closer, I smile; he smiles back. I keep on walking and hear his feet behind me. He is talking; saying what? He seemed shy at the dance, but what is he saying now, and why is he following me? Suddenly he leaps forward and is walking beside me, then he puts a hand on my shoulder and turns me around toward him with his black and red-checkered arms. I shove him away. He pulls me to him. I struggle and suddenly he pushes me down onto the hard icy ground. I try to get up and can't. 'You're a pretty girl,' he says in English.

"I can't see his face now, only two large pupils darting back and forth. He is holding me to the ground and breathing faster. He lowers his huge body and tries to put his mouth on mine. I turn away. 'No!' I say. I can't seem to get a breath with his hulk on top of me. I pound on his chest. I scream, but there is no one to hear. His body is rigid as a slab of metal; he is angry. But why? 'Don't! Don't!' I yell.

"He must have watched me leave the dance alone and followed me. I feel like a trapped rabbit. I can't move my body but I free a hand and pound on his chest and hit his face. I try not to pass out.

"He is clutching at my heavy skirt, pulling it down, ripping my coat open, then my sweater, tearing my camisole. 'No! No!' I keep yelling. 'Stop! Stop!' I feel his sandpaper hands touching me, everywhere. One hand yanks hard on my winter underwear. His other fingers tug at his own scratchy wool pants.

"I yell, 'God! God!'—or think I yell—maybe my shouting is only in my head because he has slapped one of his bear claw hands over my mouth. I jerk open my lips and bite down hard, sinking my teeth into his thick fingers. He groans and smacks me across my face and curses me in the language I don't understand.

"I am half naked on the frozen ground. His grainy rough hands are between my legs. I feel something else, hard, pushing against me. I scream, 'Don't! Don't!' He keeps pushing the hard thing and moving up, smashing down on me. He is tearing me apart. The pain rips through my body. Until he splits me open.

"I need all my strength to fight the pain. I bite down on my tongue until he stops moving. He rolls to the side of me, struggles up, yanks up his pants, buckles his belt. I hear his boots crunching away in the snow.

"I stare up at the winter sky but there is nothing to see. Only tree branches hiding the stars. The world is black and I am glad of it. I want to die from the pain and the cold."

I had never before thought of my Grandma Bridget as a young girl. Never imagined her powerless or in danger. Or attacked by a vicious monster in the woods. My body on the stairs felt icy cold, shivering inside, trembling outside. Another chill ripped across my shoulders. I crossed my arms to get warm, but it didn't help. Then I heard Grandma Bridget let out a wail and cry out: "I hadn't even had my first kiss yet."

A scuffling in the parlor told me the women had circled their friend and were bending over her, holding her in their arms. "Bridget, Bridget," I heard, then a gasp. I wondered who was crying. And then I realized that all four of them must have been weeping together.

CHAPTER 11

Hannah

I HAD PLANNED to change into my overalls after school and climb a few woodpiles at the lumberyard with my friends Connor and Brendan, but I changed my mind when Mama invited me to join her for tea at her friend Millie's. I hadn't recovered, not that I ever would, from hearing what happened to Grandma Bridget in the woods, but I hoped Mama and her friend Millie would take my mind off of it for a little while.

Millie, coffee brown hair pinned neatly back in a bun and wearing a starched white blouse, served me tea in a pink china cup the same as hers and Mama's. She offered me a butter biscuit and then asked me about school and my girl's club. Millie was Mama's best friend, I guess, next to her sister Bessie. I had always kept a close eye on Millie in case I might like to have perfect manners some day. I watched how her long slender fingers picked up her teacup as though it was a robin's egg. Ma claimed that Millie put on airs, but I say she was a born lady. I even dreamed up a story about how her countess mother had died on the ship from Ireland and how the O'Reilly family had only claimed her as their own. I was pretty sure that *could* have happened.

Soon Millie and Mama were giggling and gossiping so I gazed past the lace curtains and out a window and wondered how long Mama would want to stay. When I glanced back, Mama was taking some brownish photographs from her purse. "Look what I found in my Grandma Katie Mahaar's photo album." Mama laughed. "It's you and me, Millie, in our baby buggies in front of Ma's house."

"Who's the little girl standing behind the prams?" Millie asked.

"Oh, that's Hannah," Mama said.

Since I had nothing else to occupy me, I stretched my neck and peeked at the blond curly headed girl in the picture. "My, wasn't your sister a pretty girl?" Millie remarked.

"Half sister," Mama corrected. "Beautiful is more like it."

Half sister? I counted up my aunts in my head, Annie, Nellie, Bessie. No Hannah in the lot. When my mouth opened to question Mama, she turned and glared at me, her cheeks turning crimson. I knew enough to close my mouth, but I was certainly going to hound Mama for an explanation on the way home.

We had only two blocks to walk down Baraga Street to Ma's house, so I got down to business as soon as we had said our goodbyes and were out on the street. "You don't have a sister Hannah," I said.

"Half sister," Mama said. She kept on walking as if that was going satisfy me. I didn't even know what a half sister was.

I dove in front of her and walked backwards. "How can somebody be half a sister?"

As we turned the corner at Genesee Street, Mama grabbed me by my collar and turned me around. Tossing her head to the side and sizing me up, she said, "You're only ten and a half years old. I'm not sure what I can or can't tell you."

"But I'm smart for ten and a half."

"If I tell you this, you can never, never breathe a word about it to anyone. If you do, Ma will throw both of us into the street."

My insides did a somersault. "I won't! I promise!" I yelped.

"Here it is then," Mama said. "Hannah is actually Grandma Bridget's first daughter. Illegitimate daughter, that is."

"What kind of an answer is that?" I asked. "What's 'illegitimate'?"

"Hannah was born before Ma married Da."

I knew how babies were made, just like animal babies, so my brain immediately sprinted backwards to the terror in the woods. "When was this baby born?" I asked.

"Shortly after Grandma Bridget came back from her job at the Lumberjack Inn in Grand Marais," Mama answered.

"But she was only fourteen then." I had about a million other questions to ask, but we were already home and Mama quickly escaped me inside the house.

❦

I cornered Mama during the following days though and got her to tell me as much of the story as she and Bessie had found out for themselves. "Ma never told us anything," Mama said. "We got our information from Ma's mother, Grandma Katie, who gossiped with us a lot when we were growing up."

"So pretend you're Grandma Katie and I'm you, and tell me everything you know about Hannah."

"Good Lord, girl, you're too inquisitive for your age. Sometimes you wear me out with your questions."

Mama shot me her most wilting look, but I already knew how to tell if she was in the mood to talk. And that's when I pounced on her during the next couple of weeks. The following is what Mama told me that my Great Grandma Katie had told teenage Bessie and Mama years earlier.

To begin with, Bridget's mother and father, Michael and Katie Mahaar, took Bridget's baby girl into their home to raise as one of their own and sent Bridget, who was fifteen by then, back to work, only in town this time. The last thing Katie and Michael needed was an extra baby to feed, but Katie placed the new baby girl in a well-used basket and sighed, "Nobody will notice one more infant in the Mahaar household in any case."

When people saw the baby for the first time, they exclaimed how stunningly beautiful she was. Being the youngest, Hannah charmed the entire Mahaar family for a few years. With eight so called "brothers and sisters" who were really her aunts and uncles, Hannah might have been lost in the crowd if it hadn't been for her ivory skin, flaxen blond hair and large gray eyes that set her apart.

In the meantime, her so-called "oldest sister" Bridget seemed to pay no more attention to baby Hannah than to the rest of the Mahaar tribe. And that was a shame, because the child Hannah needed more from the woman she called Mama, than poor Katie could give. The girl hung on Katie's skirt begging for affection, but Katie was too exhausted from the cleaning and cooking she'd done all day in somebody else's house to notice.

By five years old, Hannah had become a little hellion that nobody could ignore, kicking and screaming, refusing to sit still at the table or to follow orders of any kind. Katie sent her to school to get rid of her, but Hannah spent most of her time in the cloakroom corner as punishment for disrupting the class. Every year, Katie Mahaar prayed that the four-room schoolhouse would keep Hannah another year. Finally, at the end of sixth grade, her teacher's patience ran out and eleven-year-old Hannah was expelled. Katie brought her home with little hope that she would behave any better there or be of much help either.

At the time, Katie was employed as a cook and housekeeper in the Harlow mansion near Lakeshore Park. Amos Harlow, who had built the mansion originally, had been a lumber tycoon and civic leader highly regarded by most townspeople. But his daughter Emily and her husband, Frederick Owen Clark, descendants of the Harlows and now living in the mansion, were another story. Only Katie knew how peculiar that family was at home.

"Tight as wet leather, one potato to a person at dinner, that sort of thing," Katie grumbled at night while soaking her feet in a pot of hot water. "Won't give me lunch. Have to walk home and back every noontime. They call themselves frugal. Cheap. That's what they are." Lifting her feet from the bucket and wrapping a towel around them, Katie would continue to mumble to herself after her husband Michael and the children had all left the kitchen. "Believe me, there's worse than that you can work for though. At least it's a steady job," she said for the hundredth time before dragging herself upstairs to bed.

When Hannah turned twelve, the Clarks offered to hire her to help her mother—actually her grandmother—with her chores. One morning, so the story goes, Katie had started the bread batter when Mrs. Clark came down the circular staircase in a slippery pink robe, reddish brown hair streaming across her shoulders and down her back, and asked Katie to do some errands for her in town.

Katie had been nervous the whole two weeks since Hannah had been hired. She knew asking the girl to watch the bread batter while she was gone was testing the Almighty's powers, but what choice did she have? She showed Hannah how to knead the dough when it was ready, pulled on her jacket and started toward the front door, then dug into her purse, pulled out her rosary and stuffed it into her coat pocket where it would be more available in case of emergency.

Moments later, one of Hannah's girl friends, swinging her skinny hips and whistling, snuck into the Harlow mansion through the kitchen door. "I stole a nickel from my ma for an ice cream," she warbled. "Come on with me, Hannah. We'll share it."

The words had barely rolled off her friend's tongue when Hannah grabbed the bread batter and made a dash for the new indoor bathroom. With her friend shrieking behind her, Hannah dumped the entire lumpy mass into the toilet. Before their eyes, the blob of dough expanded each time Hannah pulled the wall chain to get rid of it. Water, suddenly belching from the depths of the bowl, spurted out and across the floor. The girls leaped backwards with howls and scooted from the mansion through the back door.

Katie, puffing up the street half an hour later, stopped short when she reached the Harlow mansion. There stood Mrs. Clark, clasping her satin robe, screaming hysterically and hanging on to a porch rail. "I saw those hooligans tearing across the field out back. And I heard that girl of yours screeching at the top of her lungs: 'Did you see the look on old lady Clark's face?' Then they both fell into the high grass and rolled around. Laughing their heads off at me."

All afternoon, Katie begged the lady of the mansion not to fire her. "On condition," Mrs. Clark finally whimpered while clutching a water glass in her trembling fingers, "that evil brat of yours never sets foot within a block of this house again!"

Noting that her boss's left eye twitched un-
controllably and that her glass was having trouble
finding her mouth, Katie swung around and leaving
the room, grinned in spite of her exasperation with
Hannah.

Two years after the "toilet affair," as it became
known in the family, Katie, worn weary, handed
the girl over to Bridget, the mother Hannah still
thought to be her sister. By then, Bridget, herself
now twenty-nine, had met a fine young man and
married. She and her husband William and their
four small children at the time lived in the same
house where we all lived at the present time, only
then it was still a rambling old place with two hap-
hazard lean-tos attached to the backend.

Bridget already had a reputation as someone to
be obeyed by any children wishing to reach adulthood. And Hannah, banished from Katie's house,
was prepared to defend herself in the feared Bridget's home. Hannah settled into a tiny area at the
rear of the building that later was turned into a
wood shack. Meanwhile, the younger half-sisters,
Nellie, Annie, Barbara and Bessie, that Hannah
still called her nieces, kept an anxious vigil while
waiting for Hannah's first confrontation with their
mother.

They didn't have to wait long, only a matter of
days. Bridget had been stirring up a casserole for
dinner when Father Sheen from St. Michaels called
on them unexpectedly. Whipping off her apron,
Bridget instructed Hannah, who'd been staring out

the kitchen window and humming a tune, how to take over with the casserole.

"Do it yourself," answered Hannah, who, at fourteen, had grown into a tall long legged beauty with her fluttery gray eyes. Swinging herself around to face Ma, she further remarked, "I'm sure the priest would rather converse with me, anyway."

Nobody had ever dared talk to Bridget like that. Bridget narrowed her eyes at Hannah, and still Hannah didn't move an inch closer to the casserole dish. If the priest hadn't been in the room down the hall, Hannah would have been seeing stars by then.

Bridget smacked her spoon onto the table, stomped out of the room and down the hall to the parlor where Father Sheen sat thumping his fingers on the arm of Ma's wingback chair and chewing on a mint he'd scooped up from the candy dish on the tea table. Bridget greeted the priest sweetly while mulling over a proper punishment for Hannah's ungrateful insolence.

Over time, Mama told me, Hannah's whippings, locking her in her room or threatening to throw her to the wolves, only fed her free spirit. Hannah drove Ma further round the bend by never shedding a tear, no matter what her punishment.

On her seventeenth birthday, Hannah declared, "My future will never include cleaning other people's houses."

"Highfalutin ideas," Bridget exclaimed to her friend Molly who came visiting a few days later. "The gall of that girl!" Ma flattened a hand to her forehead. "She doesn't use the good sense God gave her. If he gave her any in the first place. Today she's off to The Paris Fashion to apply for a job. Marched out the front door first thing this morning in her best skirt and jacket with a red scarf around her neck. The Paris Fashion Readymade Women's Clothing Store, no less." Bridget frowned and shook her head in disgust. "My, what's going to become of her?" Molly asked.

A few hours later Hannah floated into the house and straight upstairs to Bessie and Barbara's room. Slapping her hands flat to her hips, she declared, "Didn't I tell you I'd get the job?"

"Showoff. You're lying," said five-year-old Bessie, but Barbara, three years older, gazed dumbstruck at gorgeous Hannah. Mama adored Hannah; she believed Hannah could be anything at all she set her mind to.

Ignoring Bessie's remark, Hannah gave them a full report of her victory. "Merna Olsen, who has somehow transformed herself from a Skandia potato farmer's daughter into a fancy sales lady in a black crepe dress, gave me a long snooty look when I asked for a job," Hannah said. "'As a clerk?' Merna asked me, nose sniffing invisible roses on the ceiling.

"'No, as a high fashion model,' I answered.

"Just then, Herby Pierce, owner of the shop, came out from the back end, took one look at me and said, 'You can start modeling tomorrow.' He removed his glasses and scratched his bald head. 'I admit I've never heard of a fashion show north of Milwaukee. But never you mind.' Then Herby Pierce gave me a big white tooth smile. 'We'll invent one.' he said."

Nobody on God's earth could talk to Hannah after that. About six months later, she met a man that Bridget nicknamed "Beau Brummel," flashy blue eyes, shiny black hair and dressed to the nines, in the tea shop at the Marquette Hotel on Rock and Front Streets. Hannah had taken to dropping in there after work wearing one of the smart outfits she'd gotten half price from her boss Herby.

Beau Brummel, sitting across from Hannah where the light from the stained glass window landed just right on his profile, informed Hannah that he was a successful traveling businessman. One look at him and everybody but Hannah suspected he was probably too good to be true.

"You're just jealous of me," Hannah answered when Bridget disapproved of Beau. "You'd have married him yourself if you'd met him before William." Everyone who happened to be in the kitchen at the time pretended shock at Hannah's statement, though most believed there was more truth to it than not.

No matter who thought what, Hannah married Beau and kept right on modeling for the Paris Fashion at St. Peter's Church luncheons and at the Women's Social Club bi-weekly dinners. On Saturday nights, Hannah, brilliant in a lace and velvet gown, and Beau, striking in his Chicago tailored suit, attended the weekly Knights of Columbus dance in a hall downtown.

Just when everyone thought Hannah couldn't possibly be any luckier, she waltzed into Bridget's kitchen one evening and announced, "I'm going to have the most beautiful baby in the whole world!"

"Oh, my God," Bridget said.

Hannah called the baby Mary Margaret, and, sure enough, she was the image of her mother, round fluttery gray eyes and all. Hannah confounded the whole family by showering every kind of sweet attention on the infant. She even bought a canary that she taught to sing and placed his cage alongside the crib where his chirping put Mary Margaret to sleep every night.

Whenever anyone mentioned how blissfully happy Hannah and her Beau were, Bridget rolled her eyes and murmured, "Hmm."

For months, the family held its breath and prayed that Hannah's good fortune would be permanent. But it seemed the minute they relaxed and switched their prayers to thanking God for Hannah's blessings, tragedy struck. What happened was so bad even Bridget wouldn't have forecast it. Hannah's baby died suddenly from a croup that was going around.

The first time Hannah went to visit the baby's grave, she took the canary with her. Sitting on the grave with the cage on her lap, the canary sang happily as ever to Mary Margaret six feet under. Hannah's Beau Brummel husband brought a camera and took pictures of Hannah's head leaning on the tombstone with her arms around the cage. This alone would not have seemed especially eccentric to our family if only she and the canary hadn't trotted off to the grave every day thereafter and continued to do so even when Hannah found out she was going to have another baby.

"Thank goodness that new baby boy was born good and healthy," cackled Bridget to Molly. "Considering the fact that mother, canary and new baby are still hiking out to the cemetery every day regardless of weather."

Katie, the grandmother that Hannah continued to call Mother, and her half sisters, Bessie and Barbara, the ones she still called her nieces, concluded that Hannah hadn't warmed to the new baby because she was still grieving for Mary Margaret. Bridget, Hannah's actual mother, extended no such mercy: "Hannah has excuses for everything," Bridget declared. "Looking for attention plain and simple, as always. She should pull up her socks and be a mother to that new baby."

Then finally Beau Brummel got fed up. "I'm done with the daily pilgrimage to Mary Margaret's grave," he announced, yanking his carpetbag from the closet and emptying a drawer full of underwear into it. "And that goddam canary chirping all night too." He threw the rest of his clothes over his arm and tromped out the front door of their little cottage. Hannah heard two days later that he had caught the train to Chicago that same afternoon.

"I'm not surprised," Bridget charged when a shattered Hannah came to the house looking for consolation. Bessie and Mama, teenagers by then, tried to comfort her on the sly, but Hannah was too devastated by Beau's abandonment and Bridget's cold remarks, which had never bothered her before, to bounce back.

Weeks later, realizing that Beau had cleared out for good with his Don Juan wardrobe, Hannah found a reason to get out of bed. She had decided to change her baby boy's name. Beau Brummel's real name was Chester Vertin, and he had named his son Chester Vertin, Jr.

"Why change the boy's name?" shouted Bridget when Hannah stopped in after returning from city hall. Hannah walked past her, and past Bessie and Mama too, and plopped herself and the baby down in a chair at the kitchen table. "Somebody get me some water," she said. Mama rushed out to the ice-box and brought back a glass of water with a chip of ice in it. Hannah gave a sip to the baby and then gulped down the rest herself.

She set down the glass and bellowed, "You lied to me. All my life you lied to me!" Nobody moved or said a word; Hannah looked squarely at Bridget. "Such a saint on earth you pretend to be!"

Still no one else spoke. "Made fun of my pretty blond hair, didn't you?" Hannah said.

"Your hair is beautiful," my mama said.

"Katie and Michael pretended all this time to be my mama and papa! Ashamed of who I really was, weren't you all? That why you shifted me around from house to house?"

Mama took Hannah's glass and asked her, "What happened at city hall, Hannah?" Neither Bessie nor Mama guessed what in God's name Hannah had been talking about.

Hannah glared at Bridget, spitting out her words. "Your name is recorded in the birth book as my mother. I read that and fainted dead away. Luckily, a strong, hefty woman grabbed the baby just before I hit the stone floor." Hannah drank half of the refilled glass of water Barbara had brought her. "Lovely! The very woman who hates me turns out to be my mother! You're all liars! I hate every one of you!" Hannah's head fell to the table and Mama rushed over and lifted the baby from her arms.

That very second Da walked through the back door. "What's the matter, Hannah?" he asked her, looking just as baffled as Bessie and Mama. He put his arms around Hannah's shoulders, raised her up from her chair, and helped her walk down the hall to the sitting room. Da wiped her forehead with his handkerchief and lowered her to the settee.

"Looking for attention, again," Bridget mumbled. But nobody responded because by then Bridget herself had crumpled into a kitchen chair and was holding her head in her hands. Seeing Ma in this state, both Mama and Bessie wondered if Hannah could possibly be telling the truth.

Hannah stumbled back into the kitchen about twenty minutes later. New fire in her eyes, she sputtered, "My baby and I both have new names. And don't think we've taken back the name Mahaar." She swung around, and pointing a stiff fin-

ger at the baby in Barbara's arms, said: "He is now
Bryan Grant and I am Harriet Grant."

Every eye was on Hannah as she spoke with a
strange new monotone voice. "I had a vision while
I lay unconscious on the city hall floor. An iron ore
boat captain appeared on my front porch. Looking grand in his uniform and standing at attention,
he proclaimed: 'Jerimiah Grant, a brave sailor who
died at sea, is your father.'" Hannah swallowed a
healthy breath of air before adding, "A *handsome*
brave sailor is what he actually said." Her narrowed
gray eyes defied Bridget to contradict her.

Knowing Hannah was making the whole thing
up about the sea captain, everyone present expected Bridget to explode. Instead Bridget said nothing, perhaps for the first time in her life. A heavy
silence hung over the room waiting for Bridget to
came back to life. "Harriet! Good Lord!" she finally
roared,. "Where did you get that? From one of your
fashion magazines?"

Hannah, now Harriet, squinting her eyes,
frowned at Bridget, grasped her baby out of Barbara's arms, plopped him onto one hip and headed for
the door. Before reaching for the knob, she flung
herself around. "Harriet Grant is a brand new person who never knew Mr. Beau Brummel Chester
Vertin. And Hannah Mahaar no longer exists." She
slammed the door behind her, the baby howled,
and both were gone.

Bridget pushed herself out of her chair, and
hands over her face, made her way uneasily from
the kitchen to her sitting room, leaving her daughters, Barbara and Bessie, to sort out Hannah's

shocking revelations on their own, which they did every night for a week. Neither girl knew what Ma had or had not told Da in the past, but it didn't seem to matter to him. The girls concluded that Da wouldn't have minded a bit that Bridget happened to be Hannah's mother; he worshiped her that much.

One thing was for certain, the new Harriet didn't dress nearly as well as the old Hannah. Harriet harbored an unshakable notion that fancy clothes had led her down the garden path with Beau. "That will never happen again," she swore.

Somehow, though, in spite of his mother's increasingly dowdy apparel and mistrust of family, Bryan grew into a fairly normal boy. The day he turned fourteen, he got himself a job after school at Getz Dry Goods and Finer Men's Clothing Store. He expected this to please his mother because they needed the money and because the store would sell him clothes at a discount, but instead, Hannah/Harriet flew into a rage at the news. "Finer Men's Clothing? You want to follow in the footsteps of that no good Dapper Dan father of yours?"

Bryan shrugged and kept the job but the first time he emerged from his bedroom, proud in a shiny new double-breasted blue gabardine suit, all hell broke loose. "Look at you!" his mother gasped, "Now you're the image of your scoundrel father!"

After this blowup, Hannah/Harriet sunk into an overstuffed chair for several days staring blankly out the window of their Pine Street cottage.

"I hear your mother's making a scene as usual," Bridget said, coming to Bryan's aid the next time she saw him. Nobody seemed the least surprised when Bridget sided with the boy against his mother. Bridget invited Bryan to tea every afternoon after school and work. "Just keep your new clothes here in an upstairs closet," she told him, pouring his tea and laying out the ginger snaps. "You can change back into your cord knickers and sweater before leaving for home."

Unaware of this conniving between Bridget and Bryan, Hannah/Harriet believed her son had quit his job at the clothing store and was staying late after school to study. She boasted while visiting at Ma's house, "Bryan and I are getting along famously these days." Nobody let on any differently, but the day after his graduation from tenth grade, Bryan, with Bridget's urging, kissed his mother on the cheek, packed his things and left town for better opportunities in Milwaukee.

Hannah/Harriet collapsed and took to her bed immediately from the shock of Bryan's departure. She quit her two-hour a day job at a Rexall Drugstore and only went to the grocery store every couple of weeks. On the rare days she emerged from bed and home after that, her clothing had gotten darker and shabbier than the time before. She passed old acquaintances on the street, head bowed, seeming not to recognize them. Barbara and Bessie, her half-sisters, dropped in unannounced to check up on her every few weeks; otherwise, she stayed away from family.

A few years after Mama and I had come to live at Ma's house, Bessie spotted Hannah clumping up the Front Street hill on a hot summer afternoon wearing a long black frock and an oversized pair of men's goulashes, unfastened and flapping onto the cement as she walked. Bessie followed her from a block behind, all the way to Hannah's Pine Street house, and was shocked to find that sometime during the previous two weeks, all of Hannah's windows had been plastered with newspapers from the inside.

Bessie tried the front door but Hannah had already bolted it from the inside. She pounded with no response, and then ran all the way home. Dashing upstairs she called out to Barbara. "I have something terrible to tell you about Hannah." Secluding themselves in Bessie's room after supper, they made secret plans to try to save their half sister.

The next day they made the first of what became weekly treks over to Pine Street. Again, having no luck rousing Hannah, they left the bag full of bread and tins of food they'd snuck out of Ma's pantry beside the front door. They waited a half hour behind bushes across the street in case Hannah should retrieve the groceries, but her door remained closed.

After that, the girls were relieved to find that at least the food they had brought the week before had been taken in. On one occasion, when Barbara and Bessie arrived, Doris Johnson, an elderly neighbor across the street, called out to them. A few minutes later, huddled together on a love seat in the Johnson's tidy ornate living room, Doris told them a story that chilled them to the bone:

"A few days ago," Doris began, straightening her delicate frame as if for courage in a chair opposite them. "I saw Hannah's bolted door fly open. A second later, I watched her soar from her porch. Her high black-laced shoes skimmed over the floorboards. Her long black skirt flared out at the hips. A black shawl flowed away from the back of her head and shoulders looking every bit like a hawk taking flight. She scurried to the center of the road and stopped short. Next thing, she started swaying to and fro. And then." Doris quit mid-sentence and took a breath before going on. "I swear this is true. Hannah suddenly stopped swaying, lifted her head and gazed directly into the sun. Then she let out a wail, shrill as a wounded animal's." Mrs. Johnson paused to address the young women again. "Do you want me to go on?" she asked.

Bessie glanced at her older sister. "Yes," Barbara said, clearing her throat, "We're both in our twenties now, quite mature enough."

"If you're sure," Doris said. She adjusted her glasses before speaking again.

"Hannah stood motionless for several minutes after that. Then whirling her body in a circle twice, cape and skirt swirling around her, she threw her shoulders back, held her head high and marched from the center of the road back to her yard and onto her porch. She pushed her front door open, took a satisfied glance back at the street, and yanked the door closed behind her."

"Lord Almighty," Bessie yelped.

Barbara dug deep just to find her voice. "Thank you for the story, Mrs. Johnson. Can we go now?"

They held hands all the way back to Ma's house hardly speaking. Even hours later in Bessie's room, they barely discussed what they had heard from Doris Johnson. Finally, Bessie asked, "Do you think craziness runs in families?"

Barbara answered, "Of course not. Don't be silly." But neither of them slept much that night.

A few weeks later, Bessie and Mama viewed the same scene for themselves from behind a bush in front of the Johnson house. They decided not to announce their presence, out of respect they told each other, both knowing the real reason was fear. As soon as Hannah was safely inside again, they set their groceries on her porch and raced home.

In spite of Hannah's present life as a hermit, even Bridget hadn't expected her to end up in the middle of Pine Street moaning at the noonday sun. Bessie and Mama prayed nightly for their half sister's return to sanity, and also, since sanity seemed unlikely, for her safety.

"I think Hannah's daffiness started with that chirping canary in the graveyard," Bessie said one night sitting next to Mama on our bed.

"Lord, Bessie," Mama disagreed. "Hannah didn't need a canary to send her round the bend. She knew that neither Katie nor Bridget had thanked the Almighty for His blessings on the day she was born. And she didn't have to go to city hall to find out that Bridget resented her. A child knows those things. Hannah knew."

"This howling at the sun is Hannah's final decline into hair-brained lunacy," Bridget proclaimed to all three of her cronies who had squeezed themselves onto the front porch swing one afternoon. "Hannah's outcome shouldn't have been a surprise to anyone. Her father was a beast, wasn't he? We tried to help the girl. She never appreciated anything."

Molly reached over and touched Bridget's hand. Liddy said, "Awful thing from the beginning."

Mary sighed. "Dreadful for everyone" Then first glancing warily over at Bridget, Mary added, "For Hannah, too."

"In the name of the Father and the Son and the Holy Spirit," murmured Bridget, shooting her right hand to her forehead, then to the center of her chest, then to the right breast, then to her heart.

Bridget may have hoped that spelled the end of Hannah, but Hannah lived on for years, performing her mysterious rite whenever the notion struck her.

The rest of Hannah's story I know for myself. Mama and Bessie continued their food missions to Pine Street every week. And, since I now knew the whole story, Mama let me accompany them sometimes and one noontime I viewed her black cape streaming behind her and her skirt slapping the road beneath her boots with my own eyes and with my own ears heard her cursing at the sun. I thought about Hannah a lot after that when I was alone in my room—especially after a day when Ma had been hard on me. I understood Hannah's anger at Ma. Hadn't I felt the same way toward Ma or Willie? I had often felt like an oddity in Ma's house the way Hannah had. And to be truthful, I was glad to find out I wasn't the first to get her ears boxed by Ma. Hannah's story made me ask myself if the whippings I got were entirely my fault. Maybe Ma was still mad at Hannah when she boxed me.

If I believed that, didn't I have to allow that Bridget had some reason to resent Hannah, the baby who took away her childhood and who would always remind her of the horror she suffered in those woods that night?

In fact, I started to wonder if our family stories ever had endings. Maybe one member simply passed his or her grudge on to the next person in line, Katie and Michael to Bridget, Bridget to Hannah, Hannah to her son Bryan, Bridget to me, Willie's dad to Willie, Willie to me. Instead of blaming each other, I wish we would blame bad luck. I mean the bad luck of being poor. I've seen people in our family turn furious, sometimes mean, from the weariness of working their bums off just to make a sorry living. Instead of getting mad at each other I wish we would pitch a fit of anger at the real cause of trouble and do something about it.

In the name of Hannah, maybe.

CHAPTER 12

Summer of 1912

PRACTICALLY ON THE same day the last of the snow melted that spring, Uncle Jim showed up at our door. What a pleasant surprise for me because I didn't even remember I had an Uncle Jim. He was Ma's oldest son, Mama's oldest brother, who had left home before I was born. You can imagine everybody's amazement when he turned up after nearly fifteen years. And just before my graduation from sixth grade. He said he timed it that way and then winked at me. And, wasn't it better to concentrate on Uncle Jim than remain so gloomy thinking about Aunt Hannah?

Since nobody ever got to sit on his or her hands in Ma's house, the household conversation switched immediately to finding Uncle Jim a job. Ma, who was never happier than organizing other peoples' lives, led the discussions. Then one evening she made an announcement at the dining table. "I've come to a conclusion," she said. "I think Jim should be a businessman." Her words hung in the air halfway between the boiled cabbage and the potatoes, leaving everyone at the supper table too dumbfounded to speak. Uncle Jim, however, kept right on eating his sausage and potatoes as though Ma was talking about somebody he hadn't had the pleasure of meeting. Or else, he was smart enough to know a good thing when he heard it, and to keep his mouth shut.

Ma wasn't the least discouraged by the silence that greeted her bulletin. "I'll have to give the subject a little more thought," she admitted and that was that for the time being.

"Ma must have won the Irish Sweepstakes," Mama told Bessie when they were safely upstairs. "How else is she going to turn Uncle Jim into a businessman overnight?"

"Maybe she found a bit of Dominic's train robbery loot in the Copper Country woods," Bessie said and Mama laughed. They were always fantasizing about tromping through the forest and tripping over a pile of the old payroll gold that had spilled out of the bag or about taking a train to Minneapolis, demanding Dommy's share of the booty from "Lucky" Eddie Hogan and living glamorously for the rest of their lives.

As for Uncle Jim, Bessie and Mama agreed that Ma would pull a rabbit out of a hat somehow. And, sure enough, at the end of the week, Ma clinked a spoon to a water glass at the dining table and declared: "Jim has a contract with the city to pick up garbage from the entire town." Nobody dared ask how she had managed this miracle. Mama always said it was best not to hound Ma for details. This must have been one of those times, because the family and boarders alike smiled approvingly, no questions asked.

The following week Ma sold a portion of her lot to a neighbor who had been pestering her to buy it so he could enlarge his own barn. With the profits she bought Uncle Jim a team of horses and a freshly painted red dump cart. "So now Jim is a businessman," she announced at the table that same evening.

Uncle Jim, a tall, husky man with a full brown beard, went straight to work building extra stalls in the carriage room and piling hay and supplies in the loft. He parked the empty wagon in what space was left in our back yard and was ready to tend to his business affairs by the following Friday. Watching him hustling around the barn, I got caught up in the excitement of all this activity occurring in my own backyard. My brain cells whirling like snow in an upside down paperweight, I wondered if there was some way this unexpected turn of events could lift my spirits a bit more.

And then one night in bed after saying my prayers, I got this brilliant idea. The next day I ran home at noontime and caught Uncle Jim just as his team of horses and dump cart clopped into the back yard after morning pickups. "Hey, Uncle Jim," I hollered " any chance you could give me a ride back to school after lunch?"

A toothy smile broke out above his lovely beard and he answered, "Sure thing." I felt crummy then because Uncle Jim didn't know what I had in mind.

Not crummy enough to give up my plan, however. I jumped proudly from the seat next to Uncle Jim to the grass and marched into school without explanation to any of the kids in the schoolyard.

The next day, as I'd expected, those who'd seen me dropped off the day before, along with others, straggled into our backyard at lunch time. Uncle Jim howled when he saw them. "Okay, climb in," he called out, motioning for them to pile into the back end of the dump wagon. A few bigger kids pulled up the younger ones behind them until they had all squeezed in. As soon as we were well out of the yard and heading down Genesee Street, we started to sing: "Row, row, row your boat gently down the stream," and didn't stop until Uncle Jim pulled his team up in front of the school and we all piled out.

It was a glorious set-up for as long as it lasted. I was crown princess of the sixth grade for exactly two weeks until our teacher got wind of it. With a room full of kids smelling like garbage from Scandinavian, French Canadian, American Indian and Irish homes, I really mean *got wind of it.*

"Well, guess that's the end of our free taxi service, Ruthie," Uncle Jim said, like he was really sorry. What was the point of telling him that it wasn't exactly "free?" Three pennies each wasn't enough to mention to a businessman like Uncle Jim, was it?

Before I knew it, sixth grade graduation was over and school was out for the summer. I got up with Mama at six o'clock every morning to finish my chores by noon so I could have a few hours in the afternoon just for me. I had plenty of kids, girls and boys, to play with, but the boy games were more fun. I wasn't mad about cowboys and Indians cause you always knew who was going to win. Run sheep run, hide and go seek, and pompom pull away were my favorites.

Unless I could persuade my friend Teresa to join me, I was the only girl who gathered with the boys in an empty field to play baseball a couple of blocks from our home. We weren't supposed to hang around there but Billy Morrison, the cop on the beat, only chased us away if it was past nine o'clock curfew time. Sergeant Morrison singled me out for the same lecture every week: "Ruthie Hogan. Your Grandma would have hysterics if she could see what a tomboy you've become." He smiled when he said it like he was only doing his duty and covering his bum if Ma found out where I was.

So I always smiled back and answered, "Yes sir, Officer Morrison."

Uncle Jim and I had breakfast together most mornings cause we both got up early. "Say, Ruthie," he said one morning. "If you finish your chores by noontime, I'll take you with me on my rounds this afternoon."

"Will I?" I leaped at this chance to find out more about Uncle Jim.

We pulled out of the yard after lunch with me sitting next to him on the driver's bench. "I'll keep my lips sealed if you'll tell me the truth about where you've been for the past fifteen years," I said right off.

He let out a yelp. "The truth, hey, Ruthie?" He stroked his beard thoughtfully. "Let's see. Should we start with my trip to China in a cargo ship or my camel ride across Afghanistan?"

I was too flabbergasted to choose. I swallowed hard and squeaked, "If you ever fell in love with a princess, tell me about that first."

"Of course," he said, "She was a black-eyed Egyptian beauty."

I pictured Cleopatra's twin and a younger Uncle Jim, even more handsome than now, if that was possible. "Was she walking along the Nile when you met her?" I asked him.

"As a matter of fact that's exactly where we met. You're a smart girl, Ruthie. Let's see, you're not eleven yet. I'd better save some of the details till you're older. Let's just say we fell in love. There's no telling why, but there's nothing you can do about it when it happens. Her family didn't think I was up to their standards, however. Imagine that, and me a handsome sailor off an American vessel. In the end, the guard spied us kissing in the palace garden one night and chased me off the grounds with his sword swinging. To escape, I swam miles all the way to where the Nile River empties into the wide blue sea." He swiped his hand across his forehead and grinned at me. "My, my. She was lovely."

He told me many more startling stories between our pickups and on our way to the dump south of town that day. And plenty of other tales on other days, except for the occasional morning when

Jeannette wanted to come along. She was only two years younger than me, but Uncle Jim clammed right up when she was present. All she asked were silly little girl questions: "How much do the horses eat?" "How many miles high is the moon?" I tried to discourage her from joining us, first so I could hear more about his adventurous life and second, cause I wanted Uncle Jim all to myself.

Once I asked him, "Why not write a book about your travels?"

"Because they'd burn up the paper they were written on," he answered, then tapped the back of my head. "You know by now that I was no stranger to saints and royalty and the scum of the earth as well. I've seen the good in people and the evil in them too. Evil too brutal for most people's tastes."

"Oh," I said. "Well, I still think you should write it some day."

Personally, I'd rather have listened to Uncle Jim's tales than anything, but on some really hot days he let me off at the beach a few blocks east of our house for a swim and then picked me up on his way home. A few of my friends were usually there already. None of us owned bathing suits, so the girls wore their underpants and a slip and the boys wore knee length underwear. Ma would have had a fit had she known this, but she never found out because we built a bonfire and dried off our clothing by standing in front of it before going home.

On special days, some of us brought potatoes to roast, and, if we were lucky, one of us brought a shaker of salt and some butter in wax paper. Those potatoes were delicious after a cold swim in Lake Superior. Once, we even pooled enough pennies together to buy a package of marshmallows and roasted them for desert—which was heavenly.

❦

Next to spending time with Uncle Jim, my greatest enjoyment, even more than swimming, was sneaking over to the sawmill down the street from our house. As many times as Ma and Mama, and even Da, had warned me not to go near the place, I couldn't seem to stay away. Once I laid eyes on those immense piles of logs in neat rows behind the mill, I had no control over my feet.

I took turns with the boys acting as a "watchout," signaling the rest when the men left the mill in the afternoon or if we sighted anyone returning. When a watchout flapped a red bandana above his head, we knew the coast was clear to make a dash into the yard through a side entrance.

I had been climbing the regular size piles since I was about seven or eight, only lately my friend Brendan O'Riley and his gang had begun to tease me with stupid chants: "Hey, Ruthie, hate to tell you, but you're only a girl. You'll never climb the tallest piles or do really dangerous stunts."

The bravest boys climbed to the top of piles as tall as a second story rooftop, only shaped like a church steeple. Then, to make the trick more thrilling, they picked the piles that were stacked in rows about four feet apart. With no running start, they leaped from the top of one pile to the next; the object was to get down from the second pile before the logs behind them started to roll faster than they could gallop down to safety at the bottom.

I watched them do this all summer, envying their courage, praying that they wouldn't get hurt, and thanking the Almighty for saving them when they escaped by a hair. I wanted to do that stunt so badly the center of my belly ached for it. Every morning I got up hoping that that would be the day I'd be fearless enough to do it.

One afternoon, I sauntered over to the lumberyard and Brendan yelled at me from the very top of an immense pointed stack. "Ruthie, come on up and enjoy the view."

I knew by the wide smile on his freckled face that he was only rubbing it in. Everybody knew a girl had never jumped one pile to the next in all history. All the same, I knew at that very second that today I had to do it, even if I walked on crutches the rest of the summer. A drum beat louder and louder in my ears until I felt like a Fourth of July firecracker with a lit up wic.

My legs, moving faster than I'd taught them how, sprinted up, up, up, one log to the next. I didn't dare look backwards at the sawdust floor.

The next thing I knew I was staring square into Brendon's eyes, round and bright as two cat's eye marbles, his mouth hanging open like a hungry dog. "Jasus, Ruthie, what the hell got into ya?" he yelled.

"I wanted to wipe that smile off your face, that's what," I said, and then sucked a big gulp of air to keep from fainting.

"I hope you're still laughing when you reach the bottom," Brendon said, trying to act cheeky, but I noticed his complexion had gone pale under his freckles and his voice sounded worried. "You want me to come after you, or me to go first?"

"I'll go first," I said. If I didn't outrun the logs, if this is how my life should end, what difference did it make who went first?

"Watch out!" I hollered, then leaped across the divide and landed hard like a two ton elephant on the pile four feet away. With my feet on fire, I bounced one log to the next starting down the pyramid. Come what may. I heard Brendon yell behind me and then a blast of thunder and the screaming sound of bark scraping against wood and logs slamming one against the other.

At the bottom, the difference between living and dying would be clearing the avalanche long before your head could tell your legs whether to dive to the left or right to get out of its way.

Surely I'd sprouted wings because the next second I soared through the air to the left, not one second before dozens of logs rumbled one atop the other toward the bottom, then, landing with a thud, they crashed to an abrupt halt. I whirled around to look for Brendan and couldn't see him anywhere, then heard his voice blasting out from the other side of the downed logs: "Jasus, Mary and Joseph, Ruthie, you're gorgeous!"

I ran out and around to the right and saw Brendan jumping and hollering his head off and we both fell to the ground and rolled over and over hugging each other until our ribs ached.

A dozen or more kids who had seen the whole thing, whistled and cheered us like wildcats. Brendan bowed swinging his hand in a circle and touching his toes like a musketeer, so I joined him with a sweet bow of my own.

That night, long before my heart rate had returned to normal, I wrote in my diary: "July 15, 1912. I did the most dangerous stunt of all. And lived to tell about it. I think even Hannah and her spirits were rooting for me. This is the best summer of my life! And it's not over yet!"

CHAPTER 13

Ma's Finest Hour

FROM THE AFTERNOON that Ma came huffing and puffing into the kitchen with news that even *The Daily Mining Journal* hadn't printed yet. "Straight from the horse's mouth," she declared to Bessie and Mama who waited breathlessly to hear the rest of Ma's latest bulletin.

"Which horse's mouth?" asked Bessie, forgetting for a second that Ma never snitched on her horses' mouths.

Ma slapped her pocketbook on the table. "The Cleveland Cliffs Iron Company is going to finish constructing the pipeline and standpipe to supply electricity to the Upper Peninsula and the iron mines by the end of August. Out on Highway 41." She tossed her hands up and out to the side, palms up. "So we've got work to do."

Sitting in the corner of the room churning butter, I was all ears, pretty sure that Ma had more interest in this event than mere electricity. "You really seem excited, Ma," Mama said, reading my mind.

"Cleveland Cliffs is bringing half a dozen of its own electricians and engineers here for the whole month of August to supervise the end of the project." Ma waited a suspenseful moment before coming to the point for her dumbstruck daughters. "Well, they'll have to board them somewhere, won't they?"

Looking more confused than before, Bessie said, "But we have no empty rooms, not even an extra bed."

That was true, but all four of us in the kitchen knew Ma would pay that little fact no mind. Her face still aglow, she looked like somebody who believed her ship had finally come in. "All professional men," she gushed. "Imagine what we can charge a rich company like the Cleveland Cliffs for *professional* men?"

According to Ma this is what happened the next morning. Ma got herself gussied up and Da took a day off work to cart her seven miles over to the nearest Cleveland Cliffs office. Da waited outside in the buggy while Ma climbed out, straightened her skirt and clopped up the four stairs to the front entrance. Once inside, she told a baffled receptionist, "I'm hear to speak to the manager about an important matter."

Thoroughly befuddled, the trim young assistant shot up from her chair and escorted Ma straight into the office of Jack Bergstrom, the District Manager.

"Please sit down, Mrs . . . ?" said an astounded Mr. Bergstrom raising his tall lanky form to its feet behind a grand mahogany desk.

Ma plopped into a chair facing him as he sank back down, his inquisitive eyes peering at her above wire rimmed reading glasses

Quickly introducing herself, Ma wasted no time getting down to the business at hand. "I hear you will need a place to board the six engineers who are arriving to finish the pipeline and power plant. If you want the best boarding house in Marquette, lovely, clean, best food in town, you'll have to make reservations for your men now." She crossed her arms across her chest. "Or, you'll miss out. This is a very busy time of year for letting rooms."

"How did you know about the engineers?" stammered Mr. Bergstrom. "We haven't even announced completion of the project to the public yet." He raised one eyebrow. "I mean, nobody knows." Having no intention of declaring her sources, Ma simply smiled while he fidgeted with his fountain pen. "Well," he said, leaning back in his leather chair and giving Ma a long look. "What do you charge?"

Without blinking an eye, Ma answered, "Thirty-five dollars each a week." Since this was twice her usual price, she sweetened the pot with a lovely broad smile.

"I'll have to think about it," said Jack Bergstrom scratching his forehead. "Sounds reasonable, though."

"More than reasonable," Ma said. "And you're smart to make reservations for the rooms before the men arrive."

Mr. Bergstrom rose up from his chair "Ah, well, I didn't intend to . . ."

"Oh, you won't be sorry," Ma said, springing up from her chair. With her purse under one arm she reached the other hand across his desk and shook his hand. "So nice to meet you, Mr. Bergstrom. I'll send you the contract in the mail."

He struggled to stand again, but by then Ma had turned to leave. As she skirted out the door, she pretended not to hear him slide back into his chair and mumble, "What the devil...?"

Ma tripped down the outside steps, a sly grin on her face. "Well, William," she said as Da helped her into the carriage, "by the end of August, we'll be on Easy Street."

Da gazed at her in admiration. "Brilliant, Bridget. Maybe we'll vacation in the South of France this fall then." He touched her cheek and laughed, moving closer to her while flicking the reins. "Now, where in the world will we bed down six men, never mind set their behinds to eat?" They chuckled all the way home at how they had outwitted the big shots.

The next morning after breakfast and the current boarders were out the door with their lunches, Ma trotted next door carrying a platter of donuts to visit Mrs. O'Brien, our neighborhood snoop. Half an hour later she returned carrying an empty platter in one hand and a lease to rent Mrs. O'Brien's basement for a month in the other. "There's a faucet in the corner of the cellar for them to fill their pitchers and washbowls, and they can use the O'Brien outhouse, of course," she stated. As though that settled any problem she could possibly have.

"We don't have room at the dining table," Mama offered cautiously.

"We can rent another table from the used furniture store down on Washington Street," Ma shot back. This was before Ma had partitioned off the end of the dining room to install a bathtub, so there was still plenty of room for an extra table. She shrugged her shoulders and clapped her hands. "Beds, running water, privy, food. What else do they need?"

That afternoon Ma called on all of her cronies to borrow spare furnishings from their attics, then ordered Uncle Jim to bring his wagon around to their houses to pick up the donations. By nightfall, she had scraped up from the cronies and the used furniture shop three full size beds to sleep six men, six washstands, each with a porcelain pitcher and bowl, another dining table and 6 wooden chairs. Uncle Jim stacked everything in our back yard and did a little no-rain dance he claimed he had learned in Africa.

Before starting breakfast the next morning, Ma corralled every family member living under her roof—Da, Uncle Jim, Uncle Danny, Mama, Bessie, Willie, me, and even little Jeanette—together in the kitchen. No question, this was serious business: even the quilting bee preparations hadn't called for a special meeting. Mama dragged me out of bed and nudged me down the stairs. "For heavens sake, hurry, Ruthie," she scolded. "Ma's recruiting another army this morning."

Grandma Bridget ordered all of us to sit down, then strolled back and forth like a General briefing his troops. "Our first order of business is to clean up that filthy, musty cellar and smelly outhouse next door. I need a good worker at my side to get that done properly." I breathed a sigh of relief. From Ma's viewpoint, that would let me off the hook for sure. I was hardly listening, in fact, when she said, "So Ruthie and I will handle those chores."

I darted a look at Mama who raised her shoulders, obviously as shocked as I was by Ma's choice. By then, Ma was assigning duties to the rest of the clan. I tugged at Mama's arm when we trudged back up the stairs. "Kiss me goodbye, Mama. I'll be dead before the month is out."

"But, Ruthie, didn't you hear what Ma called you? A good worker." That point hadn't hit me, but now that I thought about it, it was probably my very first compliment from Ma. Then and there, I decided Ma wasn't going to have any reason to carp at me for the rest of her life by telling everyone I'd let her down in her time of need.

An hour later, I was leaning against Mrs. Busybody O'Neil's cellar wall and choking on air smelling worse than a moldy vegetable larder. All I wanted was to get out of there without getting sick. I wasn't about to do anything to discourage Ma though, and adding my puke to the present odor, would definitely put her in a bad mood. But how in the name of St. Jude was she going to make this medieval dungeon livable in three days?

Ma scampered down the cellar steps then, and rushing from one twelve inch ground level window to the next, forced them open as if that was going to turn the place into a rose garden. All afternoon we scrubbed down walls, swept cobwebs from the ceiling, and swabbed the cement floor. When the floor had dried, we threw clean, borrowed rag rugs over it. Next, Ma signaled the family men as well as the regular boarders to haul in the furniture from our backyard.

"Not there, here. . . . No, we need a washstand on both sides of each bed. . . . The bureaus against the wall!" Ma issued her orders while Da and his pack of laborers hoisted and shoved obediently. When they finished, Ma and I were alone again. We made up the beds, spreading bright colored quilts from the cronies over them and shoving scrubbed chamber pots under them. I thought that was the end of it, until Ma opened another box, reached inside and pulled out pictures of birds in carved wooden frames bluebirds and robins and canaries, you name it. She told me she'd won them at a church bazaar two years earlier.

We hung all twenty-four of them here, there and everywhere, me handing Ma the pictures, Ma smacking nails with a hammer into the unpainted rough wood walls. "There," Ma declared standing back about a foot to admire our work. "They won't notice the ugly walls now," she said.

Naturally, I smiled in agreement, but in my opinion, if I were to have those stupid beady-eyed birds on their perches watching me all night, they'd be carting me off to the asylum in Newberry the next morning.

"Come on, Ruthie," Ma said. "We earned ourselves a cup of tea." It was already five in the afternoon, and I was tired enough to fall asleep on one of the rag rugs, but I followed Ma back to our own kitchen. After all, you never knew; I might not get an invitation this good from Ma for another eleven years.

She poured tea and got out the ginger snaps and chatted away with me like we'd been the best of friends all along. Before I knew it, I caught her mood and was telling her about school and Teresa and Brendan and my other friends. I felt almost as warm toward her that minute as the time on the farm when we'd sat close together in the shade of the big oak tree having lunch.

Two days later, early in the morning, when the six company engineers arrived in clean shirts, fancy ties, pressed pants and shiny shoes, I was so nervous for Ma I could hardly say, "Glad to meet you."

Ma brought them over to their quarters in the cellar like she were welcoming guests to Buckingham Palace. She bragged about the running water faucet and fresh air coming in the open windows and how they would have breakfast every morning and a packed lunch to take to work and a hearty meal in the evening. At the finish of her speech she took my hand and we backed our way out the door and up the stairs. Feeling her palm wet with perspiration, I knew she had been as scared of their reaction as I was. Before we reached the middle cellar step we heard one man say, "Well, it's not big city accomodations. But this is fine for a month. Near the job and all."

"Sure. What else do we need?" asked another.

I looked up at Grandma and smiled and hoped she knew I was really proud of her that minute. "Worked out all right, Ruthie, didn't it?" she said still holding onto my hand.

Each morning after our new boarders had left for work, I scurried next door to empty the chamber pots and slop jars first thing. Ma and I made the beds together and once a week, we changed all the bedding and replaced the soap and towels on the washstands. The rest of the chores were split up. Bessie and Mama cooked the lumberjack breakfasts; Bessie packed lunch pails and Ma and Mama cooked the hot supper as usual. The grown women took turns doing laundry and tucking clean shirts and underwear into the men's bureaus every day. I did most of the dishes and kitchen cleanup, and Jeanette emptied all the wastebaskets.

As usual the men, especially Willie, got off nearly Scot-free. Oh, Willie got stuck with the milk-maid chores, but that was about it. For a change, I didn't spend a penny's worth of time worrying about Willie. I had Ma all to myself. I overheard her in the kitchen after supper one night telling Mama and Bessie that I was a first class helper. Do you think I cared anything about that lazy slouch Willie after hearing that? I knew Ma's sweet attitude toward me wouldn't last forever, so I sopped up every bit of it while I could.

Near the end of the big shots' stay, as I was carrying out a chamber pot, Ma, looking war-weary but pleased, waited for me outside at the top of the cellar steps. "You know something, girl?" she said. "We've earned more money in the past month than we usually do in six months. And now, I have some good news for you."

"What, Ma?" I sputtered, my hand shaking so bad from anticipation I was afraid I'd spill the pot.

Ma smiled, shoving her shoulders back and suddenly looking taller. "Here it is. I've asked a seamstress over on Genesee Street to make you a plaid skirt and a matching red jacket to wear to school in September."

Stumbling on the last step but still holding onto the chamber pot, I screeched, "Oh, boy. Honest? My first readymade clothes!" Not something made from old clothes my aunts had worn out is what I thought, but didn't dare say.

"You earned it, Ruthie," Grandma Bridget said. "I've always told you God rewards hard work, haven't I?"

The ending to this incredible summer was to be a picnic to celebrate completion of the electricity standpipe. I begged Mama all morning to let me wear my chore overalls so I could have more fun. Finally she gave in, mainly because she and Bessie were too busy getting prettied up for the big event to fuss at me. Before they stepped out the door that morning in their long cotton skirts, puffy sleeved blouses and wide brimmed straw hats trimmed with new ribbons and handmade flowers, Da smiled at them proudly and told them. "You're more fetching than any two models on the latest cover of the McCall's Pattern Book."

Ma, Mama and Bessie rode in the buggy with Da because they were in charge of bringing our picnic food; the rest of us walked the three miles along the beach to the picnic spot where we had a nice view of the standpipe. It was a glorious, not too hot—not too cool, day with lots of sunshine.

Due to my usual expert eavesdropping earlier, I had a hunch that Mama and Bessie planned to escape from the rest of us after our picnic lunch. They believed I was too young to know what had been going on since our boarders arrived, but I'd have had to be blind not to see how flustered and plain silly they'd been acting while serving dinner to our out of town guests. Whenever the two bachelors in the group teased Mama, her neck and cheeks turned bright pink and her eyes started to blink like a person about to have a seizure. All the while, she pretended not to be in the least aware of them.

Never mind, I wanted Mama to have a grand day, to be happy enough to fly like a seagull all the way across the lake to Canada and back. And also, if she were having a lovely afternoon, she wouldn't have time to keep track of me.

It seemed everybody in town who wasn't deathly ill or having a baby was there for the celebration. The standpipe had turned out splendid, standing like a tall beacon on a hill behind the prison and overlooking the sandy beach and magnificent lake. Being nearly the first to arrive, our family settled itself at a long table near the party tent. Mama and Bessie covered our table with a red-checkered oilcloth and laid out the food from our baskets: watermelon, boiled ham, cold potatoes, cabbage salad, mustard, pickles, fresh bread and a chocolate cake for desert later. The adults ate so much they had to take naps on the grass afterwards, giving my friends and me our first chance to gallop down to the beach for a swim.

With our clothes only half dried from a small bonfire, we trudged back up the hill about four o'clock just in time to hear the band tuning up under the tent. Teresa and I stationed ourselves at the side of the wooden platform where we could have a good view of the dancing.

One of the first couples on the floor was Ma and Da, waltzing together, a long slide in one direction, then the other. I didn't even know they knew how to dance. Next came Uncle Danny with a chubby French girl he'd met at St. Michael's Church. Then, to my absolute astonishment, Uncle Jim suddenly appeared from behind a nearby tree with a curvy lady, frizzy blond hair and eye makeup, on his arm. Where had he met such a woman? Not in Marquette, I was pretty sure. She could have been from Chicago, or New York . . . or, come to think of it, Paris or Russia, maybe Austria. He hadn't told me about her, but I certainly intended to ask questions tomorrow. I couldn't take my eyes off of them gliding across the floor and laughing. But how could she breathe, much less laugh, with him holding her so close to his chest?

And then, oh, my God, no, came the cronies, one by one, dragging husbands behind them. I ducked behind a tree and howled till I was too weak to stand up. Teresa hooted with me and we both fell to the grass. Every time I howled, Teresa shrieked louder until we sounded like a couple of daffy dogs barking at the moon. "Quit it," Teresa sputtered, shaking her long black hair in my face. "I'm going to faint in a minute."

At last pulling ourselves up from the grass, we crept back to the dance floor and then stopped dead in our tracks. There on the floor was Mama, her white skirt whirling about her, cheeks a rosy color to match her blouse, straw hat dangling from her shoulders at her back, eyes glittering like two black diamonds, in the arms of tall, broad shouldered Mr. Andrews, one of our two bachelor boarders. It seemed to me that everyone was watching my beautiful Mama and the dark handsome engineer from Detroit, but they seemed unaware of anybody but themselves.

I could have gazed at them forever, spellbound, my body top to bottom tingling from the pleasure of it. And at the very same moment I knew that I would never forget this day in 1912 and my wonderful summer of miracles.

CHAPTER 14

The Hooligan's Revenge

SCHOOL STARTED THE way it always did in September with me crossing off the days until my favorite holiday, Hallowe'en. I loved Christmas, the lights and the tree and luscious dinner and the new diary I got from Mama every year, but nothing could ever measure up to Hallowe'en. Concentrating on fractions and geography and book reading all day was pure torture while anticipating the lovely rotten things that might transpire that evening. This year was no exception; I got in trouble twice with my teacher, Miss Maki, for humming a tune and wiggling in my seat while she was at the blackboard.

I had to rush through the boarders' supper cleanup in order to meet Teresa and Brendan in front of our house by eight o'clock. Teresa insisted that we all hold hands on our way to the empty lot. "Don't be a fraidycat, Teresa," Brendan barked at her impatiently, "We walk this street every day of our lives."

I could tell that Teresa was annoyed at Brendan for his remark. Nevertheless, she kept a tight grip on his hand. Teresa was like that, always seeing shadows behind bushes and houses even when it wasn't Hallowe'en, for heaven's sake. One time, to stop her shaking and whimpering, I had thrown rocks at a supposed monster by a tree and she squealed that I had hit him bulls-eye between the eyes. This night, being Hallowe'en with only a sliver of a moon in the sky, I had to admit that I was a bit nerved up myself by the time we met the rest of our gang at our abandoned field.

We bundled our heavy coats around us and squatted in a circle in the long grass, then took turns telling ghost stories that were so worn out we laughed instead of shivering with fear. But suddenly, Teresa of all people, stood up, her black eyes piercing the dark, and started in on a brand new story. "This is a true tale told to me by my grandpapa," she began. I wondered if it would be an Indian or a French Canadian story, because Teresa, being a half-breed, had one Indian and one French grandpapa.

We didn't wait long for our answer. "Most people know that Indian tribe elders rise up from their graves on Hallowe'en, then spread across the countryside in celebration of the new harvest," Teresa said. Then, pausing, she rolled her eyeballs 360 degrees as if contemplating whether or not to carry on. "Ordinary white folks, however, are unaware of the fact that the minute the elders have left the burial grounds, young fallen braves carrying big grudges against the white men claw their way out of the freshly opened graves as well."

With a bellowing from her throat that sounded more like an ailing bear than a pretty French Indian girl, Teresa raised our fannies four inches off the damp ground. "Beware not to cross them, for they will haul you back to the burial ground and suck you into their graves faster than you can yelp, 'Mon Dieu!'"

Again, Teresa hesitated a moment. No one took a breath until she opened her mouth again. "You will know the grudge holders are nearby when you hear the sound of howling bobcats in the distance and see faint smoky forms swimming across the land. Getting closer and closer. And closer and closer. And closer. By the time you feel their long slender fingers at the back of your neck and a fiery breath on your face, it's too late to worry."

The sky had gone pitch black by now. "Believe me," groaned Teresa, "these restless souls have stored up enough anger to bury the whole group of us six feet under without a second thought." Teresa snapped her finger and thumb in the air. "If the notion should strike them."

She swung her head swiftly in the direction of a patch of sand on our baseball diamond. "Look over there," she pointed. "You see them creeping toward us now?" All eyes shifted toward first base, and, sure enough, I saw, clear as my own shaky hand in front of me, gray silhouettes shimmering above the ground in their buckskin suits, floating toward us.

"Quiet! Listen!" Teresa moaned for a full minute. "To the shrill cries of the bobcats. They're
getting nearer," she screeched. "Nearer! Almost,
almost here!"

I leaped to my feet. "I hear them. I hear the
bobcats!"

Suddenly, Teresa pointed furiously toward
third base, screamed, buckled over and fell to the
ground. I ran over to her, dragged her by her shoes,
and then, grabbing her hand, lifted her up and
shoved her ahead of me, both of us stumbling out
of the field. With Teresa practically in a trance,
it was up to me to save us both. All the same, I
looked over my shoulder and was pleased to see the
boys, with Brendan in the lead, hightailing it down
Genesee Street as fast as we were.

I bundled Teresa up our front stairs so Ma
wouldn't take notice of her transfixed state. Once
Teresa and I were in my bedroom, I brought her
back to life by telling her, "Teresa, you scared the
bejasus out of the boys."

"Non! Vous et crazy! I did? Oui?"

"Yeh!" I yelped, and Teresa fell over backwards
onto the bed and we both rolled over each other
and howled and roared some more till we nearly
fainted from exhaustion.

When we had collected our wits, we meandered
down the hall, waltzing round and round on the
way. Hearing Mama in the kitchen, we bounced
down the stairs. Mama made us a cup of tea and
set out some ginger snaps. Pretty soon Ma walked
into the room and joined us. You never knew with
her; you just never knew. Then Mama, to my sur-

prise, nudged Ma and asked if Teresa could stay the night since we didn't have school the next day. Ma sighed. "If you want to sleep in one bed with these two giggling maniacs, that's up to you, Barbara."

We finished our tea and Mama went out to mail a letter she had written to her new bachelor friend, Mr. Andrews, in Detroit, and then to visit her friend Millie down the street. Teresa and I went back upstairs and on the way, overheard voices in Willie's room. Since Uncle Danny had gone out for the evening, it would have to be Willie and his hooligan friends plotting their evening.

Hugging our bodies to the wall and pressing our ears to Willie's door, we tried to make out the words. As we suspected, Willie and his gang were planning shenanigans. "You'd think they were getting ready to attack the British Army instead of deciding whose windows to soap and which street signs to knock over," I said, poking Teresa. Teresa giggled and I told her, "Shhh!"

Teresa and I crept back down the hall to my bedroom, leaving the door open a crack so we could hear when Willie and his mob emptied out of his room. Ma's house had gone perfectly quiet and dark by the time the hooligans shuffled out and down the back stairs. Then we heard Willie sputter, "Here we come, Stingy Louis."

Upon hearing Stingy's name, Teresa and I rose up from the bed, ripped our jackets from pegs on the wall, pulled them on over our nightgowns and were out the back door, neither of us speaking a word. Old Man Stingy Louis was the most hated person in our part of town. He owned a business at the top of Genesee Hill, a combination grocery store in his basement and wagons and horses for hire in a barn out back. He employed the youngest kids he could find to do his hardest and filthiest jobs after school, knowing they were thankful to earn any money any way they could. Then, at the end of the month, when they held out their hands for pay, Stingy often handed them a skimpy bag of wilted vegetables and a few tins of food from his shelves instead of the promised coins. Stingy even tried to pay off his adult delivery drivers that way when he first hired them, but their boss tested the wind with his middle finger and they all stomped off the job. Stingy's real mistake, though, was pulling this on Willie once, because, as everyone knew, Willie never gave up a grievance.

Teresa and I forgot that we were out past our curfew for twelve year olds and under, and that an hour earlier we'd been scared out of our wits. Chasing after Willie and his brigade of troublemakers, we stayed far enough behind not to be detected, but close enough not to miss any of the action. They added four or five more ruffians to their band on every block. By the time they reached the top of Genesee Hill they numbered about twenty.

Stingy must have heard a rumor of trouble, because four cops were already stationed in front of his house. Everybody knew that Stingy got more window soapings than anyone in town. Why not? He had more enemies than anyone else. But this time, plowing into the back yard, Willie's battalion headed straight for Stingy's outhouse. Teresa and

I watched from the shadows of an oak tree as the fourteen, fifteen and sixteen year olds piled their bulky bodies one against the other and leaned on the outer rear of the shack.

"Heave Ho!" they yelled, all at once shoving with all their weight once and then once again. The outhouse upended with a blast, then crashed forward and collapsed into an oversized box of spilt matchsticks.

"Cripes," hollered Willie as the open hole began to exhale its rotten fumes into the air. Coughing and shoving each other out of the way, the huskies slapped one another on their shoulders and backsides like a pack of howling wolves.

Teresa and I, mouths opened wide, were speechless, having just witnessed the best show of our lives. But half a breath later, we knew it had only been a first act when Willie's mob surrounded Stingy's "wagons for hire." Four or five boys grabbed hold of each wagon from the front end, yanking and pulling, and next thing, dragged all four wagons out to the street.

I expected the cops to swarm over the lot of them and shove them all into a paddy wagon parked out front, but then I spied Billy Morrison, our neighborhood officer on the beat, leaning against the side of Stingy's house and watching as if he were at a picture show at the Delft Theatre. I caught his eye, and then, remembering that I was standing there big as life in my nightgown and slippers, wanted to faint dead away from embarrassment. I held my breath for a second and then, to my shock, saw that Officer Morrison was sending me a big friendly smile. I nudged Teresa and she waved at him and then he gave her a sly grin too. Then it dawned on me that there might be no love lost between Stingy and the cops either. So Teresa and I hustled ourselves out to the street for a better view of the excitement out front.

By the time we reached the front of Stingy's house, Willie's gang had already positioned four wagons at the top of Genesee Street, the hill that didn't end until it reached the railroad tracks at the shore of Lake Superior. Four boys, screeching and hollering, stood behind each wagon. Willie shouted orders, his good arm swinging in the air like a one-armed orchestra conductor. "One, two, three," Willie yelled above the noise. A second of silence followed before Willie yelped, "FOUR!" And all four wagons were set loose. Gaining speed every inch of the way, wooden wheels squealing with each turn of their rims, wagon bodies bashing against each other, they headed straight down the steep hill toward the lake.

All four colliding near the bottom at the railroad tracks, two crashing head-on, one somersaulting, another performing a perfect canonball over the other three, the wagons thrust onward. Like a herd of buffalo sprouting wings, the wagons soared over the embankment, diving one by one into the black waters. Submerging, rising and bouncing to the surface, submerging and rising again and submerging one last time, they got swallowed up finally into a pool of bubbles.

An eerie second or two of silence set in at the top of the hill in front of Stingy's house, then roars and clapping and cheers broke out and Teresa and I hugged each other. Most of the crowd rushed toward the band of hooligans to congratulate them. A line was forming to shake Willie's good hand.

Something told me that this might forever be the best day of Willie's life. His face exploded in a cheek-to-cheek smile, his jacket threatening to pop its buttons. And wasn't I standing there, furiously clapping my hands along with everybody else? Just as if my cousin Willie had never ever whacked me, or snitched on me, or lied about me or hadn't always been Ma's favorite at my expense.

Willie glanced over at me that very minute, and even then I didn't stop clapping. Then I smiled at him. I couldn't stop grinning, in fact. Imagine me rooting for Willie. Better yet, now Willie smiling back at me?

CHAPTER 15

The Trouble with Being Twelve

THE FIRST SNOWSTORM swirled in off the lake two weeks after Hallowe'en. By Thanksgiving, our town lay nestled comfortably under a blanket of snow. We kids waited anxiously for each new snowstorm to cover the old with a new layer of powder and for the layers to build to a foot-deep solid carpet on the roads, soon to be ready for bobsled coasting. As always, I watched this transformation with relish but for the first time ever, my attention was being yanked in another direction as well.

Every two years Rosie Jansinian, an Armenian dressmaker and cloth peddler, came to town, and this was her year. Our three local readymade clothing stores sold suits, coats and serviceable dresses to those who could afford them, but most people made their own everyday clothing. Mrs Jansinian, on the other hand, offered our townswomen their only chance to get themselves a fancy dress for special occasions. Rosie turned out gorgeous frocks: ankle-length, high-necked, sleeves puffed to the elbow, tight at the wrists. And when the dresses had been fitted and sewn, she decorated the women's wide brimmed hats with flowers and feathers to match their new outfits.

The last time Rosie had come to the house I was only ten, and the women fussing over fabrics and styles had seemed downright foolish to me. But this time I was anxious to let my fingers roll over Rosie's colored cotton and linen materials and to find out which fabrics Ma and her cronies and Mama and Bessie would choose. I even wanted to take a peek at her fashion magazines. This both surprised and annoyed me, and I kept hoping I'd get over it because I didn't want to have to choose between dressmaking and bobsledding. That would be most confusing. Strange, how everything had seemed so clear cut before I turned twelve.

Luckily, Rosie Jansinian arrived before the roads were bobsled ready. She had regular customers all over town, but in South Marquette, Rosie did all her business at Ma's house, staying with us night and day for two whole weeks. Ma brought Rosie so many customers—her married daughter Annie, Ma herself, Mama and Bessie, Ma's four cronies plus women from the neighborhood and church—that Bessie and Mama suspected Ma got a discount for her own family's apparel. Ma never owned up to this, but I couldn't imagine Ma *not* turning Rosie into a lovely opportunity.

In some ways, Rosie and Ma were a lot alike. Rosie had come to America from another country the same as the Mahaars and the Hogans, but I was pretty sure a place called Armenia would be more mysterious than Ireland. Perhaps princesses and princes living in marble palaces as in "Ali Baba and the Forty Thieves" stories. I loved to listen to Rosie speak English with her strange accent, but I was surprised to hear her tell Ma once that she had a hard time understanding Ma's "brogue." Ma didn't have an accent, did she? Maybe she did though; cause her mother Katie surely did.

But how would a person like Rosie Jansinian learn to be a fashion expert, turning rolls of fabric into marvelous dresses "without ever using a pattern," as Mama claimed? Maybe in one of those palaces using only golden threads and silk and velvet cloth? Or she might have been born with the talent, like artists and poets and musicians. In that case, she could have taught herself. They say anybody could have talent, even me. If so, mine certainly hadn't shown itself to the sunlight yet. Just as well. I was far too busy at the moment for talent.

Mrs. Jansinian arrived on the first morning with her usual grand supply of materials: bolts of cotton and linen heaped so high she needed two horses to pull her wagon and three boarders to help her haul in the material. Rosie, a tiny lady with a mop of curly black hair hanging loose at her shoulders, breezed in the front door, sat down at the kitchen table, served herself coffee and helped herself to a donut. Gulping down a second coffee and two more donuts, she and Ma caught up on family news while Bessie and Mama snatched up Rosie's style magazines. Rapidly flipping pages, they squealed over artists' drawings of the latest London and Paris fashions. Then they got up and pawed through the rolls of material, groaning with delight over this one or that one.

Mama got her heart set on a bolt of cream colored linen right off. "Bessie, give a look!" She rolled her fingers over folds of the fabric holding a corner up to her fair complexion and dark hair for Bessie to test the contrast.

"Ohhhhh," Bessie sighed.

"There you go, Barbara," Ma criticized from her seat at the table. "Wanting the most expensive and impractical of the lot. And there's Bessie looking at a nice green durable cotton. She may be younger than you, but she has a lot more sense."

From my spectator position under the dining room archway, I'd been listening to Ma insulting Mama in front of Rosie, when, to my astonishment, Mama actually spoke up. "This is the one I've chosen," she said, giving Ma a sassy look over her shoulder. "And I'm going to stick with it. I'm paying for it, aren't I?"

I nearly faded dead away. Mama must have wanted that creamy linen more than the remainder of her life. I wanted to run over and hug her for being so brave. At the same time, I was imagining the two of us out in the street by nightfall again.

Ma gave Mama a look that could have wilted rosebuds on the vine, but still Mama didn't move an inch from her chosen bolt of linen. Instead, running her fingers over the creamy folds, she kept murmuring, "Ummm. Ummm." I figured she was picturing herself in a luscious creamy white suit with her hand looped over Mr. Andrews' arm, sashaying down a Detroit promenade.

Rosie pushed away from the table and rushed to Mama's side. "Fine choice, Barbara," she said, clutching a stylebook at the same time. "Now, let's find a style worthy of this marvelous cloth."

For the first time in my memory, Ma let the matter drop then and there. Well, almost. Realizing she'd lost out when Rosie took Mama's side, Ma somehow managed to turn the whole thing around to make herself seem the heroine of the day. Later, some of the people present swore Ma had been the one to suggest the creamy linen in the first place.

Poking at the material, Ma admired the texture while contributing her two cents as to the proper style for such a luxurious fabric. Bessie and Mama ooohed and aaahed over the books until more women arrived bringing fresh baked goods to the table. Soon, they were all behaving as if this were Christmas and St. Patrick's Day rolled into one. "Haven't had this much fun since our last wake," said Ma's old friend Molly. A worn out joke, but they howled like it was fresh off the press.

By noontime, Rosie Jansinian's scissors were cutting cloth into patterns of her own design. I begged Ma to please let me watch Rosie at work. "Only if you promise not to run off at the mouth every minute and not to get in Rosie's way."

I waited till Ma left the room before questioning Rosie: "Why cut the material sideways?" "Will you show me how you make buttonholes?" "Can I pick out the buttons for Mama's dress?"

Watching Mrs. Jansinian perform like a magician all afternoon, taught me one thing for sure: If my talent ever decided to come out of hiding, it would not be as a seamstress or dress designer. First, my fingers were too clumsy. Next, I couldn't sit still long enough to make all those tiny stitches. And third, I couldn't sweet talk those silly women all day. And fourth, you had to be an artist like Rosie—which I wasn't.

That night, gazing out the window at another day's snowfall, my thoughts ricocheted back to visions of bobsledding. I didn't regret watching Rosie work; or seeing Mama with cheeks bright and chin out standing up to Ma. But, whew, I was grateful the coasting hadn't started without me. The guys would have never stopped ribbing me if they'd heard I was visiting with the sewing lady instead of joining them on the hills. I was one lucky girl that the snow packed hills had waited for me.

Word swiftly spread through school the next day that tonight would mark the start of bobsledding. With Ma and Rosie and the last of the women being fitted in our parlor, I wrapped up in my leggings and mittens and cap and snuck out the back door after supper cleanup without Ma's usual safety and curfew lecture. By eight o'clock, I stood at the top of Genesee Street hill, slick and white in the moonlight, the evening's snowfall untouched. The few cars in our part of town steered clear of the coasting hills in winter, for their own safety as well as ours.

The best coasting started at Altamont and Genesee, and, standing there at the top, I looked down at the four most gorgeous and steepest coasting blocks in our town and in all of Michigan, and probably in America. My insides did a triple somersault. Genesee, being the steepest, was reserved for the big bobs that had already congregated at the top. The young men and boys who had built their own bobs from wood planks three times the length of a davenport and attached huge coaster sleds to each end, stomped their feet to stay warm and boasted about past feats.

Being only twelve, I was too young to be a regular rider on the big bobs, but I had purposely worn a red chook in case I might get chosen to be somebody's headlight. One in a million chance of that, but when I saw handsome Denny Madigan standing tall and proud by his bob, I ran over and smiled up at him. "You did a lot of work on your bob since last winter, Denny," I told him.

Denny didn't answer, but why would he with a half dozen nineteen year old girls his own age hanging on his every word? "Oh, Denny, I know you'll be winning tonight." "Denny, how would you like for me to make you a hot chocolate after the race?"

I wanted to kick each of them in the shins, but I was too busy grinning up at Denny myself and asking questions. Finally, Denny smashed the snow with one of his boots. "Holy Mother of God, Ruthie Hogan, will ya shut up if I let ya be my head-light?"

"Would I?" I said, backing away from him with my hand clamped tight to my mouth. Then I looked over and saw my pal Brendan climbing into the front sled on Frankie Moore's bob. With his red hair and red freckles, Brendan wouldn't even have to wear a red chook. I waved at him and he signaled me back. Neither one of us had ever been a headlight before, so I knew he was as scared as I was.

I climbed into Denny Madigan's front sled try-ing hard to look confident, and then made the mis-take of looking down the hill again and to the lake beyond. Suddenly my body, head to toe, felt like rubber, but there was no backing out now. Frankie Moore's bob with Brendan in front was situated about a yard away from ours. Brendan gave me a sa-lute and I gave him one back, like we were two old veterans at this. Now it was certain that our two bobs would be first to try out the hill that winter. Knowing what an honor that was would have para-lyzed me if the start-keeper hadn't just blown his whistle. I didn't have time for anything then but flattening my body, belly slick to the sled. I hung on to the side slats and prayed. "I'm an idjut, Lord, but all the more reason to save me, isn't it?"

Denny yelled, "Go!" from the rear of our bob and his four teammates shoved the back end with all the strength God had given them. Running to keep up with our bob, all four leaped onto the back end of the sled at the very last possible moment to join Denny already on board.

A second later we were flying too fast for my mouth to suck in a breath. Snow blasting up from in front of us turned to wet crystals sticking to my eyes and nose and lips. Only then, was I startled to note that we had slid ahead of all the other bobs, so my bright red knit cap was now the only thing warning any cars coming at us from a side street to get out of the way. And then another fact slapped me in the face: *I would be the first person to reach the bottom that winter; the first to test the ice at the end.*

After the first block, I heard people at the sides of the street yelling, but I couldn't see them through the crusted snow over my eyes. For all I knew, our entire crew had flown off the rear end and I was performing a solo act.

We had to be closing in on the finish with seconds to go. Then, I heard our team yelling from the back end, "Drag! Drag!"

With my icy mitten, I scraped the crust from one eye and saw that we were still lunging forward fast toward the railroad tracks and the slick embankment at the end. As we smacked onto level ground, all I heard was the screeching and the crunching from five pairs of heavy leather boots behind me digging in and dragging through foot-deep layers of solid snow.

"Holy Father!" I screamed as we veered abruptly to the right, scraping and scraping, then towards the left, scraping more. It seemed another five minutes before we finally jolted to a sharp halt. I crossed myself twice to be sure.

Brendan's bob screamed and dragged to a stop a couple of seconds after ours. "Hey, Ruthie, we made it! Ain't we just too grand?" he hollered.

"Did you ever doubt it?" I yelled back, but Brendan knew I was full of the malarkey. I was only thankful I hadn't wet my bloomers from the terror.

"See you tomorrow night," Brendan called out to me. I didn't know how I could wait that long to ride again. If it hadn't been almost curfew time, I'd have got right back on that bobsled for another chance to kill myself. I trudged home praying now that neither Ma nor Mama would find out I'd been promoted to headlight.

That night under my quilt, I set my mind loose to imagining myself the best living bobsled headlight on earth. Being famous, I would be honored worldwide, invited on safaris to the Belgian Congo, presented tickets to sail to China and Siam and India and Europe on luxury ocean liners. Just as my brain was getting really creative, Mama came into the room and got in bed. I cuddled up to her, aching to tell her about my thrilling evening. Instead, I asked her how her suit was coming along. Mama was just as excited describing her new garment as when she talked to her friend Millie about Mr. Andrews. And that's pretty excited. Her suit sounded so wonderful that I wanted to see it that very minute. "You'll have to wait till morning, Ruthie," Mama said. "Go to sleep now."

I lay there with my eyes closed, picturing the dress and reliving the bobsled ride. I was happy I'd gotten to watch Rosie perform her talent on her sewing machine. And excited to be the first to ride Genesee Hill that winter, too. It's a good thing I didn't have to choose one over the other. How could I have given up either? If growing up meant choosing one thing over another I might not be ready to grow up yet. It was too confusing. Mama was already asleep but I reached over and caught the corner of her soft flannel nightgown between my thumb and finger and held on to it most of the night.

CHAPTER 16

An Unlikely Truce

MAMA, WITH MA'S permission, let me go coasting nearly every night that winter providing I'd finished my chores and lessons. And luckily for me, they never found out I was a headlight. While my life seemed to be getting better by the day, Willie's was heading in the opposite direction. He was becoming a handful, picking fights on the street and sloughing off on his chores, and Ma didn't know what to do with him. She had run out of tutoring possibilities, and at fifteen, Willie couldn't do much to earn a living either. Finally, Da wrote Willie's father to tell him the situation was desperate: that they needed his help with the boy.

I hardly recognized Willie's dad when he reappeared at our door; Thomas Gummerson hadn't been back to see Willie in several years and this time he stayed in Marquette barely long enough to ask one of his old big shot friends at the South Shore Railroad to give Willie a job. The friend agreed; Willie's father shook Willie's good hand, said "Good luck," and left that same afternoon on a train back to the small town on the Mesabe Range where he now lived with his second wife and two small daughters.

I think Willie tried to keep the station clean and swept and orderly as the stationmaster instructed, but he had trouble figuring out which job to do first. When he finally decided, he couldn't seem to finish with it before the next passenger train arrived. After a few weeks the stationmaster called Willie's father to inform him that he was sorry but he would have to let Willie go.

Furious, Willie's father blasted into Ma's house a few days later. "Bridget, I'm not going to pay his way any longer." He spat out the words. "I've paid his room and board here for years and he can't even keep a janitor's job. I'm finished with him. He's fifteen. Let him get a job and try to keep it."

Ma sputtered, "Where is he going to live?" Now Ma was worse off than before because she wouldn't be getting room and board money for Willie, and she couldn't continue to feed and bed a lad who ate more than any of the full-grown boarders.

"Tell *him* to find a place to live," Thomas said. He left without even saying goodbye to Willie.

Ma walked the floor in her sitting room all that night. "No use getting mad, Bridget," Da said. "Willie's father knows we won't give our own grandson to the wolves. Put the problem back on his father where it belongs. Now, come on back to bed."

"You're right, William," Ma said crawling under the quilt with Da. "What would I do without you?"

Ma repeated her conversation with Da word for word to Mama and Bessie the next morning. "I'm going to call Mr. Thomas Gummerson as soon as we finish serving breakfast," she told them.

Bessie and Mama stood beside Ma and Bessie told her, "You have every right, Ma." Ma lifted the receiver from the wall phone and gave the number to the operator.

"I've bought Willie a railway ticket to Mesabe Range," Ma lied to Thomas when he said hello.

Willie's father sputtered, "Wait a minute, Bridget," but Ma hung up before he had a chance to protest.

"Nah, I don't want to go there," Willie grumbled. Who could blame him? Why would he want to live with a father who had never in all these years come to get him? Willie was slow, but not dumb about things like that.

I figured Willie would be miserable moving in with a stepmother and a father who didn't want a big awkward fifteen year old foisted on them. How could he be an older brother to six and seven year old girls he didn't even know and who, according to Mama, had always lived the life of Riley with their engineer father?

Sure enough, Willie relayed some awful stories to Ma from Mesabi Range when he called her once a month. They treated him like a bum that might have come begging for food at a person's back door instead of an older brother in the family, he told her. "I think they begrudge me every piece of bread I eat," Willie said. "They feed me before they finish eating so I don't have to sit at the table with them. My so-called father won't talk to me and his wife gives me work orders all day long as if I was a servant in the house. I hate it here, Ma."

Six weeks after the day he had arrived, Willie walked out the front door, headed for the train yard and hopped onto a freight train. For one and a half days he hid in the boxcar, eating a bite at a time from a loaf of bread he'd stolen from his stepmother's pantry. Peering through wooden slats at the sides of the car at each stop, he listened until finally the conductor finally hollered, "Marquette Depot." The brakeman opened the boxcar doors, and Willie leaped out and ran all the way from the station back to Ma's house.

So Ma was right back where she'd started again. The very next morning she trotted down to the South Shore depot, looked the train master straight in the eye and said, "You must have another job that simple lad Willie can do. You're not going to tell me 'no,' are you, Mister Hanson? There must be something."

Jon Hanson shifted one foot to the other. "I gave him one chance already. The janitor job baffled him."

"Another chance, Mr. Hanson?"

Jon Hanson made little whining sounds like a cornered rabbit. "I suppose he could be a peanut butcher on a couple of the short runs," he said. "It don't pay much, mind you."

"Enough for room and board?" Ma asked.

"How much is that?"

"Seven dollars a week."

"Okay, I'll pay him ten a week if he's worth it."

"We'll take it," Ma said. "Can he start tomorrow?"

The household had been more peaceful before Willie returned, but for some reason, when I looked at Willie now his past meanness was no longer the first thing I saw. Oh, I was sorry I'd had to be his punching bag while Ma treated him like her personal cherub transported straight from heaven, but I felt sorry for him now. He couldn't even count peanuts easily, and half the time he gave wrong change to the passengers. I guess the finances of the South Shore Railway weren't dependent upon their peanut sales. Or maybe the stationmaster was afraid of Ma same as the rest of us; cause Willie didn't get fired. I stayed out of his way as much as possible but that was no problem because I had plenty else to do myself.

About the same time that bobsledding had run its course that winter, our skating rink froze over. The same abandoned hundred foot deep quarry three blocks from our house where older kids swam in the summer turned to solid ice four foot deep by the middle of February. The bigger boys shoveled and swept the rink smooth every evening, while the rest of us sat on blocks of granite in the warming shack fastening skate runners to our shoes. The boys who had after school jobs bought themselves shoe skates, but most of us had the regular clamp-ons. Mine had been Mama's when she was a girl, and since they no longer held onto my shoes, I tied them on with ropes.

As it happened, that winter Bessie was seeing a man friend who for some reason took a liking to me. Not only was Jean Arguenot a gentleman, more importantly in my view, he had been a champion racing skater in Canada a few years earlier. So you can imagine the astonished look on his face the day he saw my clamp-on runners, ropes and all.

"Pauvre fille!" he exclaimed, then ordered me to grab my coat and whipped me out the back door and downtown to a skate shop on Washington Street. "Fit this young lady with a pair of ICM figure skates," he instructed Eric Larson, the owner. "White, not black, and big enough to fit two pair of socks so they'll fit her for a couple of years."

Once Mr. Larson had laced and tied a bow at the top of the beautiful skates we'd chosen, Mr.Arguenot bent down to inspect the size by poking at the toes. I don't know what made me do it, but on the spur of the moment, I leaned toward him and kissed him on his cheek. "Thank you! Thank you!" I shrieked. "I never owned anything so magnificent in my whole life."

For sure, Mr. Larson was taken aback by my fresh behavior, but I didn't care one bit. If I were Bessie, I'd have married Mr. Arguenot that very day.

Figure skates! I was the envy of all my friends. I let Teresa use them sometimes, but nobody else. Getting used to the nicks in front of the blades was the hard part. I kept lunging forward and landing with my belly flat out on the ice. I practiced and practiced night after night until I got the hang of it. A month later, I don't mind saying that I was doing a decent figure eight and the swan and shoot the duck, and learning how to twirl down to the ice and back up again. Sometimes Brendan asked me to skate with him, which was nice, being old friends and all, but I was happiest when giving a figure skating demonstration in the center of the rink with everyone skating round and round me. I felt light and free and imagined myself a genuine ballet dancer.

Ma had extra guests for supper one evening, and kitchen cleanup didn't finish until after eight o'clock, too late for me to get to the rink and back by my nine-thirty curfew. I felt like a prisoner in my room all evening while picturing the clear sky, moonlight streaking across the slick quarry ice and my friends sailing around the rink. Having finished my library work and my history lesson for the next day, I paced the little room back and forth, back and forth. I pushed the windowpane up several inches to smell the crisp, cold air outside. With Ma and Da in their bedroom-sitting room and Mama and Bessie gossiping over tea cups in the kitchen, I gauged my chances of sneaking out the front door, having a few skates and coming back home without anyone being the wiser.

A second later, reaching under my bed, I grasped at my skates, ran back to the window and tossed them to the yard below. Yanking on my coat, leggings, and rubber boots and tiptoeing down the front stairs, I made a dash around the side of the house. I snuck around back of the maple tree where I was certain the skates had landed. I made a quick search for them but they were nowhere in sight. Next thing, I heard was a pair of boots crunching across the snow crust behind me. Breathing faster, I gulped hard as I turned around and faced Willie. "Looking for something?" he asked, eyes sparkling brighter than the icy crystals under our feet.

"Guess what, Willie? I opened the window a crack and my book fell smack out of my hands," I said. "Where could it be, I wonder?"

Willie slapped one of his big boots down next to one of my gollashes. "Sure this ain't what you dropped?" He dangled my beautiful skates in front of my nose.

I had no chance to turn and run before Willie burst out laughing to kill himself. "And I guess you happened to be wearing a chook and scarf and snowpants while reading in your room?"

He handed me the skates and sauntered out of the yard whistling an old sailor ditty. I stayed perfectly still for a minute or two before deciding maybe he wasn't coming back. I could have gone back inside to wait for Willie to return and squeal on me, but on second thought, I could get in a bit of skating and face the same music later. Either way, I'd get a good smacking from Ma, so I beat it out of the yard and ran all the way to the quarry.

I skated with Teresa for a while and then practiced my figure skating that was getting more superb every week. By the time Brendan helped me yank off my skates by the woodstove in the changing shack, I had almost forgotten about Willie and the punishment awaiting me at home.

When I remembered, I ran all four blocks back to Ma's house. Taking off my galoshes before opening the back door, I slipped up the back stairs. Moving slowly in front of Willy's room, I stopped to listen at his door and heard him snort and roll over in bed. Good, he was out cold. I crept the rest of the way down the hall to my room. Good thing Mama and Bessie and Mr. Arduelot had gone out to a movie and weren't home yet. All around, I'd been plain lucky. It was always better to delay a licking from Ma to let her cool off a little.

I slipped quietly into the kitchen the next morning. Sliding into my chair, I waited nervously for my punishment, but soon I noticed that nobody was paying any more attention to me than usual. Ma turned bacon in the skillet for the boarders; Mama rushed past me bringing toast to the dining room and then came back for a platter of scrambled eggs. Ma was busy for sure, but she always made time to box my ears, if that's what she intended to do.

The next thing, Willie blew into the room and pulled out a chair next to me. I scooted in my legs to lessen the kick in my shins I expected, when instead, he asked, "Please pass the butter dish, Ruthie," as politely as a choir boy.

This had to be a dream because my next thought was too daft to be real. Was it possible

Willie hadn't snitched on me? Mama smiled at me on her way back to the dining room with a jar of raspberry preserves and a water pitcher. "Have a good day at school, Ruthie," she said.

I glanced over at Willie for the first time and, I swear to God, he smiled at me, nearly as sweetly as he had in Stingy's yard on Hallowe'en. Had Willie and I signed a peace treaty when I wasn't looking? Or had he had a change of heart in that boxcar on his way back from his father's? Or could this be the Almighty's way of giving me one more chance to be a decent person?

No matter, I felt pretty good about the world all of a sudden, thinking wouldn't it be lovely if good and bad evened out like that? I spread butter on my bread, letting the idea warm me until I got a shiver remembering poor Mr. Arduelot. Bessie had told him the day before that she couldn't marry him after all. So I had the skates, and he didn't have Bessie. Now that didn't seem fair. I bit into my fresh bread where the butter had melted and then remembered how long it had taken for Willie and me to sign our invisible truce. Mr. Arduelot's good fortune could very well be awaiting him when he returned to Canada: someone to skate into the future with him, a pretty dark haired French girl from Montreal all set to fall in love with him.

I had seen enough in my twelve and a half years not to believe in fairytales, but wouldn't it be divine if things did balance out that way? Eventually.

CHAPTER 17

Lessons Learned

I GATHERED MY five best friends, Teresa, Olive, Louisa, Maggie and Myrtle together the day after I turned thirteen, which was the same day I started eighth grade. We climbed the ladder to our barn loft where we could have a private meeting. Everybody but me made herself comfortable sitting on the hay. I remained standing. "Now that we're eighth graders," I said. "We ought to do something purposeful."

Dumbfounded, all five gazed up at me. "Whaaaat?" whined Louisa.

"The other night while I was washing the supper dishes a brilliant idea popped into my head." Still nobody said a word. "I think we should claim to be a club from here on."

"Pour quoi?" asked Teresa.

Leave it to Teresa to put me on the spot. Thinking fast, I tore a page from my school notebook and ripped it into little squares. "We can vote on a purpose for our club this minute," I said as if I'd planned this all along. "Myrtle, pass your pencil around, will you? Fold your paper when you finish writing and set it on the floor next to me. I'll read them out loud but we won't know whose vote is whose."

"Why do you get to read them?" Louisa asked in her squeaky little voice. No one paid attention since Louisa found fault with everything.

I gathered them up and read aloud: "Sewing Club."

"Sewing Club." "Sewing Club." "Sewing Club." "Sewing Club." "Music Club."

I figured the last vote had been Teresa's. "Sewing club? Whatever are we going to sew?" she asked right away.

Teresa was always a step ahead of me, big black eyes putting me in a bad light. "How do I know what to sew?" I said. "I only found out the purpose of the club two minutes ago." With five blank faces defying me, I answered quickly, "Dish cloths" so I could get to the real reason being a club was a good idea.

Myrtle interrupted my train of thought. "So we'll call ourselves "The Sewing Club?'" she asked like she had just discovered the world was round.

"That seems like the right name, Myrtle," I said to her. "And now that we're a club, we can ask for certain privileges. We can meet in each other's houses. And we can have secrets we don't have to tell anybody. We can make tea and maybe our mamas will serve cookies. And then we can plan future activities."

"But aren't we going to sew?" Myrtle asked.

Except for Myrtle, the rest of the girls had sat up straighter, smiling at last. I could see they were grasping my real purpose for the club. "I bet our sewing won't win any prizes at the county fair," Olive said, grinning slyly.

At our original actual meeting, held at Louisa's house, we agreed to our first future activity, a thirteenth birthday party for Myrtle. "Why *my* birthday?" Myrtle asked.

"Because the next birthday would be Olive's and that's a whole month away." Maggie tossed her long braid off her shoulder impatiently. "Who wants to wait a month for a party, Myrtle? Not me."

Myrtle slid down in her chair and Louisa whined at her. "Don't be a baby, Myrtle."

I still had to talk Mama and Ma into letting us have the party at our house, because the members decided we had the best house for a party. I asked Mama first so she could ask Ma. "Only if you start right after school and are finished before we have to start cooking supper for the boarders," Mama answered me.

I caught her in the morning midway up the front stairs on her way to make up beds. "By the way, Mama, we're inviting boys too," I said, offhand, as if it was an afterthought.

Mama answered hurriedly over her shoulder. "What? No rough house in the parlor, Ruthie. If the boys start wrestling, Ma will toss their bones out the back door before they can beg for mercy."

"I promise," I said. "No wrestling. You won't have to spy on us at all."

Mama slapped her hands onto her hips and zipped around. "I'm not dying to spend my two hours off with a dozen thirteen year olds, Ruthie. Don't you dare get me in trouble with Ma." Mama scurried on up the rest of the stairs. At the top, she called down to me. "If Myrtle's mama can send over some cakes, I'll make the tea."

"Whew," I whistled on my way down the hall. "That was easier than I expected."

At our next meeting, Olive proposed that we play post office at Myrtle's birthday party, and Teresa suggested that we vote for the boy who was the best kisser the next time we met after that. And then Louisa whimpered, "How will we know since none of us has ever been kissed?"

"Don't worry, we'll know," Olive answered knowingly as usual. None of us ever doubted Olive's information. Olive had started to round out in ways that humbled the rest of us. Also she had suddenly started to walk differently, swinging her hips slightly every other step in a way that gave her a certain authority.

One by one, the boys arrived in Ma's parlor. I had been the calmest one in the room until I greeted Brendan at the front door; only then did it hit me that the bottle might choose Brendan and me during one of its spins. I felt suddenly faint. How could I kiss my old pal and buddy? How could he kiss me? I was sure we would both fall on the floor howling. Or if we made ourselves do it Brendan, thinking I'd become just another silly girl, would never see me the same way again.

We intended to get down to the business of parlor post office as soon as all the guests arrived. The boys stumbled in one by one until they were all seated in the parlor, legs stretched out and big feet plunked down on Ma's best weaved carpet. Club members stood in the center of the room explaining the rules of the game, except for Maggie, who giggled so bad we told her to sit down and put a hand over her mouth.

Then Olive marched everyone into the hallway to spin the bottle, first to a girl, then to a boy. Olive kept the hall door open a small crack to make sure the couple kissed when they were alone in the parlor. Too bad for Olive that the first couple chosen was Teresa and Timmy O'Neil, because Teresa spotted Olive's glittering eyeballs behind the crack at the door and bellowed, "Fermet la porte! I won't do it till you shut the door!"

That ended Olive's peeping, but we teased each couple as they shuffled into the parlor and I held my breath each time the bottle twirled until the dreaded moment when it stopped in front of me and then got spun again and shimmied slowly to a halt pointing to Brendan.

I slouched behind Brendan into the parlor, feeling more scared than before I had leaped from the highest lumber pile or headlighted straight down Genesee hill. The parlor door closed behind us and I said, "Hey, Brendon, they won't know what we're doing in here." I tried to sound chipper, but what was the good of trying to fool Brendan? He could see that my face was on fire, cheeks burning with embarrassment.

"Brilliant, Ruthie," he said, his own complexion matching his red hair.

"We can make kiss noises and pretend," I said.

He came closer to me so we could giggle nervously as we had heard the others doing. Brendan put his hand under my chin and crossed his eyes and made a silly face. I was supposed to laugh but instead, before my brain could make sense of it, I put my mouth on Brendan's mouth just to see how it would feel. Before I could decide how it felt, Brendan was pressing his lips on mine. He kept them there nearly an eternity and I didn't push him away. My body danced inside from my shoulders to my toes, every bit as excited as when it was flying downhill on a sled. Brendan finally backed up and gulped to catch his breath. He seemed to be in shock same as me. "Jasus, Ruthie," he said the way he always did right after I'd done something grand. I stood there like a dimwit grinning back at him.

"Whew," I said at last and he gave my arm a nudge. I guess we were both glad we had done it. And lived through it. I was also pleased now that I'd had my first kiss from Brendan rather than somebody else. As long as we could still be pals like always, of course.

I guess I was still in a dream state when suddenly I heard Mama in the hall, asking the rest, "Why are you out here instead of in the parlor?"

Maybe she had eyed the milk bottle on the floor, because a second later. she screeched, "What the devil!" and next thing she flung open the parlor door and sailed into the room. Brendan and I stood still as two marble statues.

"I'm ashamed of every one of you," Mama said, smacking the tray with Myrtle's mama's cakes onto the serving table so hard I thought the plate would crack in two.

She glared at the girls. "Disgusting. Putting your lips on their lips!" She gave the boys a look no different than the time she'd found a snake in our garden. "I know what your parents would think! I trusted you!"

Mama seemed baffled then and, not knowing what to say next, she tossed her shoulders back and shouted, "You're too young for this! Everyone of you!"

She swung around and started to leave but like an idjut whose brain had turned to mush, I called after her. "Will we be old enough next year?"

Mama turned on her heel, faced us again and threw both arms above her head. "No," she said, no trembling in her voice whatsoever. "Next year you'll be too old!"

I sunk down into the nearest chair and gave a look around the parlor. The girls stood with their heads lowered like they were studying cracks between the wood planks on the floor. And then I looked up and saw that the boys had all sat down and were gobbling up Myrtles's mama's cakes. As soon as they stuffed the last crumbs into their mouths, they got up and started to pull on their jackets.

Olive was the first club member to get her voice back. "Don't go," she said when they started to file out. "We haven't played pin the tail on the donkey yet." But the door had already closed behind the last boy before she finished.

We had nearly recovered from the shame of our first activity by our next meeting at Teresa's house. I figured the whole thing had taught us a lesson we wouldn't forget and that's what I told the girls. But, to be honest, I wasn't sure what the lesson was. Grownups kissed all the time so I didn't understand how kissing could be so shameful.

Anyway, that's not what was tugging at my spirits. I felt awful about fooling Mama that way when she had believed in me. But, since I had started the club, I felt I owed it to the others to raise our morale. "So the post office party won't go to waste," I said, "I think each one of us should describe the kiss we received." I gathered my thoughts. "So we'll be better prepared next time." Another pause. "Even if that's three years from now.

"Let's take a vote on whether or not to describe our kisses. I'll go around the room." Each hand went up.

"So," Olive counted: "Yes, yes, yes, yes, yes, and another yes from me."

I didn't know there were so many ways to kiss, unless some of the girls had thrown a little imagination into their descriptions. Even so, none of them sounded any where near as thrilling as Brendan's way.

⟲⟳

With playing post office outlawed and everyone bored with sewing, Teresa got her wish and we
soon became a music club. Luckily for us, Louisa's
mother kept a small organ in her parlor, and Teresa's father had purchased a player piano with dozens of player rolls at an estate auction. Ma still had
her piano in our parlor, of course. Louisa played
some classical pieces as well as new sheet music,
and I played whatever I remembered from my two
years of piano lessons with Professor Magnum.
And Teresa, who sang solos in St. Michael's church
choir, kept us warbling every week until we were
hoarse.

At the end of the school year, 1915, the music
club members finished junior high and were about
to begin high school in the fall. The day after eighth
grade graduation, Maggie gathered us together in
her parlor to make an important suggestion. "In
my opinion, " Maggie said, "any respectable high-
school club ought to have a treasury."

"But where would we get money to put in a
treasury?" Louisa wimpered.

"Lots of places," I said, before I had thought of
even one.

Olive rose from her chair and strolled to the
center of the carpet. "I have an excellent idea. We
could have a dance at the end of the school year
for students starting high school next fall." Olive grinned happily before astonishing us further.
"With actual musicians and charge admission," she
said.

The idea having come from Olive, nobody objected. In fact, everyone suddenly was an instant

expert on how to conduct a dance properly. That's when Olive took over again. "Since none of you has ever been to a dance, let me explain. First thing, we'll have to find a place to hold the dance. Leave that to me. I just happen to know that Mr. O'Reilly rents the loft over his grocery store at the corner of Third and Rock Street cheap for parties and dances."

As usual, we were amazed at Olive's knowledge of mysterious information that no one doubted for a second. Teresa said, "My papa knows musicians who need the work and will play for cheap. They have a pianist, a violinist and a drummer. The drummer visited Papa the other night, and ma mere invited him to stay for supper because he looked hungry."

Louisa tapped her fingers on the table next to her. "But can they play music for dancing?"

"Oui. Tres bon," Teresa assured us and we named Teresa music director immediately.

Olive was the only friend of mine that Mama had ever disapproved of. Whenever I asked her why, she gave me the same answer: "Because her older sisters, Mary and Margaret, have bad reputations."

"That's not Olive's fault," I argued every time, but Mama had this idea that bad reputations were like contagious diseases that Olive could catch from her sisters and I could catch from Olive. I wasn't supposed to be seeing Olive outside of our club, but all that amounted to was Olive and I meeting on a street corner every morning before school.

When the day of the dance arrived, Olive and I were both all keyed up when we met in the school-yard that morning. Olive kept begging me to skip school with her. "Please, Ruthie, please," over and over. Olive was an expert at skipping school, but this would have been my first time. I felt terrified, but excited at the prospect as well.

Finally, I said, "Okay. But what will we do all day?"

Olive twirled a finger in the air. "Plenty," she said. "For one thing, we can go to the two o'clock movie matinee."

"Without any money?" I asked because I wasn't going to sneak in the back door like Willie and his friends did sometimes.

Olive patted the pocket of her jacket. "We have money."

"What money?"

"The dance money," she said.

"You have the dance money with you?" I was more astounded at that than the idea of using it. I had sold the most one dollar dance tickets but, since the dance had been Olive's idea, she got to hold onto the money for us. Who would have imagined she was keeping it on her person?

"I don't trust people in my house," she confessed to me as if I'd surely understand. I didn't, but by then, it was too late to go to school. We scooted over to South Marquette Park fast as possible and hid, keeping an eye out for the truant officer. Olive reached into her pocket and counted out fifty cents of the dance money for each of us, enough for two bags of peanuts each and the movie later. We laughed and acted silly all morning, pretending we were gypsy girls who had escaped from the tribe until it was time to go to the movie.

Catching sight of the boy behind the glass selling tickets, I said "Good. It's Willie's one and only respectable friend." He wouldn't dare squeal on us, knowing Willie would beat the tar out of him. We sat in the back row eating our peanuts and giggling and talking. The movie was stupid, cops chasing robbers they never did catch, but we were too excited about the dance in a few hours to care much about what was on the screen.

In the meantime, because Olive had been absent so often, the principal had called Olive's mother to say that Olive had not shown up in class again. On a hunch, Olive's mother asked him, "By any chance was Ruthie Hogan also absent today?" Olive's mother knew I wasn't allowed to see Olive and was, no doubt, happy to give Mama some bad news about me. She called her as soon as she finished talking to the principal. "Did you hear that Ruthie skipped school with Olive today?" Olive's mama asked. Mama, not believing her, hung up and called the principal herself.

At about the same time, the truant officer spotted us leaving the movie theatre and hauled us across the street to the ice cream parlor so he could call the principal. He set the phone back in its cradle on the wall and squinted two mean eyes at us. "You two are going to be in a pile of trouble on Monday," he said.

I slipped unnoticed into the house about four o'clock, the time I would have gotten home from school. I had intended to reveal nothing until Monday and to suffer consequences then. Instead, Mama and Ma pounced on me when I opened the back door. Ma grabbed me by the back of my collar, swatted my behind hard and shoved me into a chair in the kitchen. "The principal called us. You didn't know that, did you?" She rolled her eyes and started in on her favorite lecture about Dominic Hogan and the apple not falling far from the tree. I deserved her harangue this time and might have soaked up every word of it if she'd left my papa out of it. I bit my lip to take my mind off what I wanted to say.

I wished Mama would march over and swat me good instead of leaning on the tubs and looking miserable. When Ma finished up and stomped out of the kitchen, Mama lifted her head and spoke finally. "What are you trying to become, Ruthie? Where's my beautiful, smart girl?" Then she turned away from me and hung onto the washtubs with both hands. Mama hardly ever cried, but I heard her weeping now and I wanted to die there on the spot.

Then I heard Ma's heels clicking back down the hall toward the kitchen. "Don't get any ideas about going to that dance tonight, girl. If you sneak out when nobody's looking, you don't have to bother coming back to this house, ever." Next thing she grabbed me by the hair, slapped me across the face, dragged me over to the back stairway and gave me a shove. "Stay in your room all night!"

Mama came upstairs to our room after serving the boarders' suppers as usual, but she didn't speak to me. Somehow the words "I'm sorry" were stuck in my throat. How could any words measure up to Mama's unhappiness?

She washed up in silence, then flipped around and stood over the bed where I lay with my face in a pillow. "I'm disappointed in you for skipping school, and I'm devastated that you would take what didn't belong to you." That's all she said, not even in a hard voice, before leaving to join Ma in the kitchen.

I padded down the hall a minute later to listen to the conversation between Ma and Mama. The first thing that struck me was that Ma didn't sound mad anymore. "I'm worried about Ruthie," I heard her say. "Bad things can happen to a young girl, especially one with that much spirit. Things that change a girl's life forever."

"Nothing like *that* will happen to Ruthie," Mama said, and I knew they were both remembering the bad thing that had happened to Ma when she was fourteen in the woods near the Lumberjack Inn.

One by one, that evening, the music club members came to our house, taking turns pleading with Mama to let me go to the dance. I watched each of them from my bedroom window as they left, floating away from the house and down the street in their best dresses, satin ribbons clipped to the top of their freshly washed hair.

Part of me still wanted to join them; I had worked as hard as the rest to make this a grand occasion. And yet, if Mama had weakened and begged Ma to let me go, I wouldn't have enjoyed myself. Maybe I wouldn't have even gone anyway. In the end, though, what I would have, or might have, done didn't matter because Mama stuck to her principles and I stayed home from the dance that night.

CHAPTER 18

Bringing in the Cows

OUR HOUSEHOLD HAD barely settled down from my criminal activities when Mama and Ma had their first ever down and out argument, over me, naturally. They didn't know I was in the back hall listening to them in the dining room. "She's too old to be rounding up the cows," Mama said in a stern voice as if she were talking to Willie or me, not Ma.

I didn't understand why Mama was so upset. I hadn't once objected to bringing in the cows in the two years I'd been doing it.

Most families near the edge of town had at least one cow and some chickens. Ma had rented a hilly pasture for years in order to graze all the cows at our end of town for a fee. My daily job was to take the cows out to pasture, a twenty-minute walk from Ma's early in the morning, and to round them up after school. Then Ma did the milking and straining and put the milk up in covered pails. When I returned from taking the cows to pasture each morning, I delivered the milk to neighborhood customers on my way to school and then picked up the empties on my way home from school.

Truly, I liked the job a lot better than my old job of emptying all the slop jars and chamber pots before school in the morning.

"Too old?" Ma shouted in response to Mama's statement. "She's too old when I say so. We all have to pitch in around here. Nobody's too old or too young for any job. That girl still thinks she's special. Maybe she's forgotten Dominic Hogan is her father? Reminds me of Hannah sometimes, she does."

I put my ear to the wall in the kitchen to hear them better. It wasn't the first time Ma had compared me to Hannah. I could take that, but oh, how I hated her bad-mouthing of my papa and the Hogans every chance she had. I bet I'd have liked my father if I'd known him better, and I was glad to be related to those rowdy talented Hogans.

Ma's remark must have bothered Mama too, because she shouted back, "For once, leave the girl's father out of this. Dominic had good qualities before he served time and fell in love with the barleycorn. Ruthie's a high-spirited girl; you call her that yourself. Maybe it's the Dominic in her that gives her spine that I don't have."

I didn't have time to enjoy Mama's compliment because the back door flew open and Willie burst through it. He took one look at my legs entwined, shoes lopped one over the other, ear plastered to the wall and whispered, "What the devil's wrong with you?"

"Shhh," I answered because Ma was speaking again. "Spine or not, she's going to take the cows to the hills and round them up in the afternoon. And that's that."

"Oh, no, Ma. I can't let her," Mama said.

Then Willie marched by me into the dining room. "Aw, that ain't right, Ma," Willie said. "A thirteen year old girl can't be wandering those hills at almost sundown by herself. I know the dolts that congregate up there. Not right, Ma."

Ma must have been struck dumb hearing Willie take my side, but Mama is the one who piped quickly. "That's what I told her too."

Willie's point that the pasture at sundown could be dangerous might have escaped Ma till then. Though she would never admit to being swayed by anyone, even Willie, she said, "Well, you figure out what to do with the cows, Barbara. Since this is your big idea. But remember, I want the cows out and back every day in time for the milking and canning."

Hearing Ma's skirt rustle and her feet clumping down the hall, I peeped into the dining room in time to see Mama send a smile over to Willie. "Thanks, Willie," she said.

I guess I owed him a thank you too for backing up Mama, only I still hadn't quite adjusted to the new Willie who'd returned from his father's place. I knew I was being stubborn, but I needed more time to get over all his past meanness to me.

❦

In any case, Mama hired my cousin Bud and his friend Harold Kellan to take the cows to and from pasture. That seemed a good solution except that she paid them each twenty-five cents a week for the same job I had done for nothing. "Why is that fair, Mama?" I asked her the day I heard my cousin Bud bragging about earning the money.

"Boys have to get paid for the work they do," she answered, but then she got flustered and disappeared from the room like she had a habit of doing when she couldn't explain one of life's dumb rules.

About mid-summer a fierce electrical storm descended upon us with such fury that Mama sent the boys, Bud and Harold, out to the pasture early to round up the cows. By the time they got there, however, there wasn't a cow in sight. Panicked, the boys ran all the way back to Ma's house, flung open the back door and sounded the alarm. "The cows are gone! The cows are gone!"

Ma was in a terrible state, arms flapping while declaring an emergency. "Those cows must have run off into the woods. Lord knows where."

"Barbara, come downstairs this minute," she called out from the front hall downstairs. "You know Ruthie's the only one who'll get those cows to budge out of hiding."

"Ma's right," I said flying down the steps behind Mama. "I'll find them if Ma apologizes for all the nasty things she's ever said to me," I told Mama on the way down.

"When pigs fly," Mama whispered over her shoulder and we both had a chuckle. Making a dash for the back hall, Mama took an oil coat from a wall hook and helped me into it. "The boys will go with you," she said.

"I don't want them." I buttoned the coat fast as my fingers would let me. "Those cows will stay put with the boys yelling their heads off."

I headed out the door before Mama could stop me and plowed through a half a foot of water in the streets, and, minutes later, the worsening downpour toward the hills. I'd have felt better if the thunder and lightning would only let up. The cows might not come out of hiding for the Lord himself with lightning crackling above them. The sky, already dark, made the path through the woods black as night.

As well as I knew those woods, they looked strange with streaks of lightning snapping on and off through the tree branches. Hoping to find all twelve cows huddled up in groups of two or three, I pulled bushes aside on the way and rummaged behind them. I called out the name of each cow beginning with our own Gracie for more than a half hour. "Molly, Trixie, Gertrude, ... come on out. I'm here to take you home."

My legs and feet dripping wet inside my boots, and my skirt and blouse soaked under the oil coat, I plunked myself down on a fallen tree trunk. I'd hardly settled my bum for a rest when I heard "Moooo" and leaped up. I ran toward the "Moooo," and, sure enough, behind a tree trunk were the loveliest pair of brown eyes ever staring back at me. As I came closer and patted her behind the ears, I explained to her what our plan would be. Finally,

Gracie inched out from behind a fat tree trunk..
"You follow me," I said, "and I'm hoping the others will follow you."

Now that I had company, I calmed down a little while continuing to call out each cow's name. Whenever I took a breath, Gracie let out a good long, "Moooooooo." At last, another cow poked her head out from behind a shrub and then another crawled out from the underbrush behind her. By ones and two's they left their hiding places and joined us. An hour later, eleven of the twelve had fallen in line behind us. The twelfth, Mrs. O'Neil's Martha, kept running away, scurrying for cover again until I broke off a switch and let her know I meant business. With all twelve lined up and following me, we started for home.

I'd been too busy to notice that the lightening had stopped until we broke out of the forest. "Thank you, Lord, for saving the thirteen of us for another day," I said feeling like a pied piper for cows as they trailed me through the streets of South Marquette.

I was plenty puffed up from hearing, "Thank you, Ruthie," every time I delivered another cow to her own backyard.

When I got to Ma's house, Willie ran out and patted me on the shoulder as if I was a soldier returning from war. Ma made me hot tea and raspberry toast; Mama stood in the background smiling so sweetly you'd think there had never been a post office party or a skipping school day or a robbery of the club's dance money. When everyone else left the room, she bent down and kissed the top of my head. "You were very brave, Ruthie," she whispered.

By suppertime, I decided the cow rescue should be taken as a sign that I was being given one more chance to avoid becoming a jailbird to become... well, I wasn't sure what I would ever become but for certain something better that where I'd been heading.

That evening Da came home from his work at the lumber mill, cleaned himself up and had his supper and then called me into the parlor. Even though I had graduated from eighth grade, he let me sit on his lap. Resting my head on his vest the way I'd always done, he pulled out his beautiful gold watch from his vest pocket and let me wind it. Then in his softest voice, he said, "I hear you did a fine job today." Then he reached into his pants pocket and brought out a peppermint roll. "Here's a present for our young heroine." He pressed it into my palm. "I'm proud of my bonnie lassie."

"Everybody says I'm a tomboy, Da."

"What's wrong with that?" he said. "You've got a sturdier backbone than a lot of boys I know, and that's good." He squeezed my hand. "That's a fact, Ruthie. It certainly is."

Opening the peppermint roll and breaking off a piece, I set the sweet hot candy on my tongue and let it stay there hoping it would last a long time.

CHAPTER 19

Talent Revealed

ABOUT A MONTH after starting high school I complained to Miss Deasy, my freshman homeroom teacher, that I'd already read nearly every book in our school library. To be honest, I really wanted an excuse to talk to Miss Deasy who was my favorite new high school teacher. She was plenty stern when it came to assignments, but she never purposely insulted or humiliated students the way some did. She greeted simple questions as if they were brilliant and then stood by a student's desk until he or she understood her answer.

"This is the kind of problem I like to solve," she said now as I watched her large comfortable face fold into a nice cushiony smile.

Ripping a sheet from a writing pad, she dipped a pen in her ink bottle and wrote furiously. When she finished, she had produced a list of twenty-five titles and authors of books, one after the other, all from memory, that I could check out of the Marquette City Library. I gazed at her in admiration.

"Now, if you have trouble finding any of these, let me know. I have copies at home you can borrow."

A week later, she asked me to stay after class. "Sit down, Ruth. I have a job I'd like you to do," she said.

I slid into a chair next to her desk, figuring she was about to ask me to tidy up the room at the end of the day or wipe down the blackboards and I wondered how I could say yes and still get home in time for my afternoon chores. As it turned out, she had something entirely different in mind. "I want you to write down your thoughts when you finish each book on your list. Tell me why you liked the book or didn't like it," she said. "Also, jot down any questions you have. I'll read your notes and we can discuss them together after school. How's that strike you?"

"Great, I'll do it," I said flattered by her request. I couldn't remember a time when anyone had ever asked for my opinion on anything. I'm not saying I didn't give it, but no one had ever actually asked for it.

"Lovely," Miss Deasy said. "Why not start with *Wuthering Heights?* Maybe a Jane Austin novel after that."

I couldn't settle down that evening with my secret assignment burning a hole in my bed upstairs. Anxious to start *Wuthering Heights*, I finished my kitchen cleanup in record time and took two stairs at a time up to my room. I'd been scribbling my life story and great ideas into my Christmas diaries ever since I'd learned to write. So maybe at least that part of my brain was alive. But what could I say about the great books on Miss Deasy's list?

Naturally, once the music club found out about my private after school chats with Miss Deasy, I was in for some brutal teasing. "Teacher's pet," they chanted at me in the school hall every chance they got. I crossed my eyes and stuck out my tongue at them and sometimes even gave them the middle finger. At last they got bored with taunting me and quit. I was as surprised as my friends, though, that I honestly enjoyed spending time with a teacher.

Then one afternoon Miss Deasy breezed into homeroom obviously anxious to quiet us down and make an announcement. "The American Legion is sponsoring a countywide competition for the best essay on patriotism," she said flailing her arms about to keep our attention. "One essay will be accepted from each high school homeroom. The first, second and third winning essays will win a new American flag for his or her classroom. So produce the best essay possible, students. We want that flag!"

No question, Miss Deasy meant business on this contest. Plunking myself down at the far end of our dining table after supper cleanup I worked on my essay every night for two weeks. Digging up facts from history books I'd found at the city library, I scribbled them onto sheets of lined paper until my fingers got stiff. A few nights later I reread my notes and fell asleep with my head on the table—they were that boring. The next day I decided that nothing I had researched was half as interesting as stories I'd heard from my own family and our boarders all my life.

That evening I pretended to be Ma and called a meeting in the dining room of all parties sleeping under Ma's roof. "There's no pay in it for you, but you can save my skin at school by helping me write this paper on patriotism," I told them, planting a pitiful look on my face for emphasis. But then, before I could even hand out assignments, they were already squabbling about who would go first, so I had them take numbers and said I'd call them in turn.

One by one, they sat beside me at the table and talked about where they had come from, telling me their reasons for coming to America and voicing thankfulness for the privilege of living here now. At the end of the week, I shoved the pile of library books and my previous notes aside and wrote their stories in their own words explaining what patriotism meant to them.

Like it or not, I handed my essay in to Miss Deasy that week. And wasn't I lucky that she did like it? I was dumbstruck, however, the next day when she chose my paper, "Coming to America," to represent our homeroom in the contest.

Imagine my greater shock a month later when Mr. Evans, our principal, tacked his notice to the hall bulletin board stating that I had won second prize in the countywide contest. I smacked my hand to my mouth to squelch the yelp about to escape. Just then, Teresa sidled up to the bulletin and let out a holler for me. Next thing, Lydia and

Olive stopped to read the notice. Mouths gapping open when they finished, Olive said, "Well, damn, Ruthie, I would have never guessed you were that smart."

While Miss Deasy was delighted that our classroom was to get its flag, in the next breath, she declared, "But those judges were dolts. Ruthie Hogan's essay should have been awarded first place. Instead, they picked an uninspired, conventional, hackneyed piece about Washington and Lincoln. There must have been no Irish judges on the panel."

Personally, I was thrilled to have won second place, but I read the first prize blue ribbon essay that evening and agreed with Miss Deasy that mine was better. Da read my whole piece aloud to the borders at the supper table the next night. Naturally, each person perked up when his own story was being read, but everyone was polite enough to listen quietly until Da finished reading. Mama clapped when he finished. Ma admitted it was good, but then spoiled her compliment by adding: "Don't go getting big-headed over this, Ruthie. I wouldn't pay too much attention to Mary Deasy. Naturally, she would think yours was best. She's as Irish as we are."

The next day, steamed by Ma's remark, I asked Brendon to read both essays and give me his opinion on the subject. I trusted Brendan because of our pact to always tell each other the truth. The following afternoon, he hollered to me all the way across the baseball field, "Jasus, Ruthie. I didn't know you could write like that. You actually *are* brilliant!"

I ran across the field to meet him, yelling back, "But was it better than the first place winner?"

"That one? Duller than reading Webster's dictionary."

Brendan's hair, ordinarily the color of a juicy ripe orange, turned fiery red in the sunlight. That moment his eyes were as blue as I'd ever seen them. I leaped toward him and threw my arms around his neck. "Thank you. That's all I wanted to know." He was so moved by my sudden passion that he kissed me good on the mouth, then and there, on the pitcher's mound in bright daylight. And the best part, neither of us was embarrassed. It was grand to have such a good pal as Brendan. Really grand.

"Guess you have to get home for your chores, hey, Ruthie?" He drew a half moon in the sand with his shoe tip. "Would be nice to walk up to the pasture and talk to the cows on such a gorgeous day, wouldn't it?" He grinned and winked and gave my arm a little punch.

"It would indeed," I said. "But I have to get home and see what awful jobs Ma has dreamed up for me."

"You coming to my baseball game Friday after school?" he asked.

"Don't I always? But it was more fun when I used to be on the team."

"Yeah. Till they found out you were a girl."

"If I'm that good, why does it matter?"

"If it were up to me, I'd let you on the team. Swear to God, I would. Even though my father would probably crucify me."

"Well, let's toss a couple of balls around Saturday afternoon. I can escape Ma for awhile about three o'clock."

"Sure," he said with a smile so broad you'd think we'd just agreed to elope together.

I sprinted the two blocks to Ma's house, bounced step by step up to my room, and yanked out my diary from under the mattress. A kiss in daylight had to be recorded while the thrill of it was fresh. Until now, Brendan had kissed me twice on the way home from skating at the quarry, and, well, several times behind the ice cream parlor after bobsledding. But never in daylight! I smiled while enjoying the moment before writing: "Everybody knows Brendan is clever in math and history and English classes. But *I'm* the only living person who knows he's a luscious kisser."

I'd barely put the essay on patriotism behind me when Miss Campbell, my English teacher, marched her tall slim body into composition class a few months later with an air of importance. Clanking her blackboard pointer on her desk for silence, she announced: "The project for the two combined English classes this spring will be to translate Shakespeare's "The Tragedy of Julius Caesar" into modern prose. We are going to use the final freshman-sophomore script as our annual theatre performance in June."

Waiting for the class to quit moaning, Miss Campbell slapped her skinny fingers onto her hips. "Those noises were rude," she said. "You're going to enjoy this work. Mark my words."

Well, the most unexpected thing took place the next day when our first class discussion on the subject began. The kids, even the boys, went wild waving hands to argue with each other, at first just for the sport of it, but actually making some good points by the end of the hour. I'm pretty sure Miss Campbell was as surprised as I was, considering the grunts she'd heard the day before. Still, she looked pleased sitting behind her desk and smiling, never once trying to bring the class to order. And this is more or less what occurred every day during the following three weeks.

On the last day of this class assignment, Brendan walked me part way home from school. "You know, Ruthie, I've decided to add seeing one of Shakespeare's plays in Chicago or New York someday to my list." He and I had been keeping lists of things we intended to do when we were grown up and had more than a nickel in our pockets.

I gave his arm a punch. "Yeh. A brilliant choice, Brendan. Let's do that before we're six feet under."

Converting a Shakespeare play into the language of 1916, however, would have never ended up on my wish list. But that didn't stop Miss Campbell from cupping her hand under my elbow, lifting me up from my desk and whisking me to the front of the classroom the next day. "Pay attention, class," she directed. "I have chosen Ruthie Hogan to translate "The Tragedy of Julius Caesar" into modern language for us. Say congratulations, everybody!"

I prayed I would pass out, or better yet, wake up in my own bed screaming, then sighing, "Ahh-hhhh! Thank you, thank you, this is only a nightmare!" But Miss Campbell had already grasped hold of my hand and was shaking it as if we were a couple of old gents meeting in a park. "You can use all of the notes from our class discussion," she chirped brightly while pretending not to notice that my body had gone rigid and was readying itself to collapse.

Finally coming to my aid, Miss Campbell dropped my hand, and seizing me with one hand on each shoulder from the rear, said, "Don't worry, Ruthie. You have the talent to do it."

"Talent?" I sputtered. "I have talent?"

Often during the next month, I wished that my talent would do me a favor and crawl back under the rock where it had resided previously. The patriotic essay had been a ring around the rosie compared with this. Sinking into the chair at the dining table again, I labored, passage by passage, page after page, my only company the creaking of old house timbers in the night. One night, holding my head in my hands and letting salty tears slide over my cheeks into my mouth, I wondered why I had agreed to this monstrous job. "As though I had a choice in the matter," I mumbled to myself before dragging my weary bones up the back stairs to bed.

The next night I was at it again and six weeks after that, feeling like a released prisoner, I presented the finished product to Miss Campbell. "Shakespeare might want to clean my clock for ruining his prose," I warned her. "But what could he have expected from a modern day Irish girl, anyway?"

Miss Campbell helped me with some changes immediately, Miss Deasy did my line by line editing and Mama performed my afternoon chores each day so I could stay late at school to watch the drama student rehearsals.

On opening night, the auditorium was packed with every student who hadn't been excused for nighttime jobs, with farm kids whose buses had stayed late for the performance and with loyal parents. I knew Da and Mama were coming, but I teared up when I spied Ma in her best Sunday dress sitting next to them in the front row.

With my name "Ruthie Hogan, Translator" appearing on the program, Mama felt obliged to scurry around the auditorium as soon as the curtain closed and the applause stopped to pluck up any discarded programs and slip them into her purse.

Afterward, Ma, Da, Mama and the six members of the music club escorted me to Donckers Ice Cream Parlor for a homemade hot fudge sundae. One after the other, the club members praised the play and swore they *had always* known

I'd had a hidden talent. I was feeling so happy I didn't even tell them they were a pack of liars. Honestly, how could they have known what I'd just found out six months ago myself?

CHAPTER 20

The Compromise

O N THE FIRST day of my sophomore year, Miss Campbell stopped me outside her classroom. Suspecting that she had another one of her "surprises" up her sleeve, my first thought was to try to escape. But she'd already captured me with a hand on my shoulder. "I know of another contest, Ruthie," she confided. "What do you think of that?"

"What's the prize?" I asked, knowing it was a brash question still, I wanted to know. Not for me: for Ma. So far, all I'd received for my hard work was admiration and I was thinking if I won something I could use, that Ma would really be impressed.

Miss Campbell grinned, then answered proudly, "The prize is six John Paul Jones Middy blouses!"

We could never have afforded to buy one Middy blouse, much less six! Ma would be floating on clouds and singing "The Star Spangled Banner" if I won.

"'The Life of John Paul Jones' is the topic," Miss Campbell said, leaning toward me to whisper as if she were revealing a national secret straight from President Woodrow Wilson. 'This one will be a real challenge, Ruthie." She frowned and shook her head. "It's open to high school sophomores through college seniors."

Suddenly, like a racehorse ready to pounce out of the starting gate, every muscle of my body went taut. Before my brain had time to say, "Nah. Not this time, thanks," my mouth was promising, "I'll do my absolute best to win, Miss Campbell."

Mrs. Ruggles, a neighbor and friend of Ma's who had been a teacher before she married, offered to help me with research of naval history at the library. At night I scribbled, crossed out and rewrote what I'd only just written. It was too ordinary and too dull, just like the first essay I had written about patriotism. I started to wonder about all this talent business. Maybe winning those first two awards had been only good luck or plain accidental. But then one morning, I bent over to tuck in Uncle Danny's clean bed sheet and an idea, so exciting it seemed to make the room brighter, the sun warmer. Before scrubbing Uncle Danny's washstand, I'd already thought of the title: "What Makes a Hero?" From that moment on, I began leafing through biographies and history books to pick out sections I liked. Then I fit them together to tell John Paul Jones' life story the way I wanted to—as a thirteen year old boy apprenticed to a merchant ship and then sent to sea in the brig *Friendship,* until, as a young man of twenty-one, he received his first command on the brig *John* that led to a long career at sea, including command of the Bonhomme Richard on which he issued his immortal words: *"I have not yet begun to fight."*

Trying to imagine John Paul's childhood dreams, I wondered on paper if he dared think he could be a hero one day. Or, had he only surprised himself by rising to an occasion when it called for heroism? As a youth, had he set a mark for himself and gone after it tooth and nail? Or, did he act where others might have feared danger or failure? Is it what a person happens to do at the moment he faces trouble, or has a person's own past already trained him to act heroic?

"A little of each of these things, I concluded at the end of my essay—for John Paul Jones, other well-known heroes and ordinary people as well. And yet, none of us knows if we have all or any of these qualities until the moment we are called upon to act heroically. Some will and some will not rise to the occasion.

With college students participating in the contest, I ought to have accepted that my chances of winning were slim. But the whole time I had worked on the project, a voice kept whispering in my ear: "Keep at it, girl, you're going to win this fool contest." Once the entries were in, though, I let myself consider the possibility I might very well lose. Whenever anyone mentioned the contest, I shrugged my shoulders and answered, "Wasn't my luck going to run out sooner or later?"

Then one evening Da glanced up from his news-paper and told me, "Your life won't be ruined if you do lose this contest, Ruthie. It's the trying that matters." He gave my hand a squeeze. "However, if I was a betting man I'd put my money on you walking away with the blue ribbon, Bonnie Lass."

"Thanks, Da," I said edging closer to him on the parlor settee to enjoy the scent of his lavender face soap and the sweet aroma coming from his pipe.

The next morning I woke up with Mama's voice in my ear: "Ruthie! Ruthie! Listen!"

I rolled over and rubbed my eyes. "It's too early to get up, Mama."

Wrapping both arms around me she brought me up from my pillow. "It's Da. Something's happened to Da." She stroked my hair and my cheek while clearing her throat as if the rest of her intended words had got stuck in her windpipe. Finally in a hoarse voice she said, "Da went to heaven during the night."

"To heaven?" I searched Mama's eyes, red and swollen, and pressed myself against her with my head snuggled into her shoulder. "You mean Da died?"

Mama nodded yes, and I opened my mouth to scream, "No!" but I couldn't make the tiniest sound. Finally I whispered, "He wasn't sick last night," as if then she would suddenly realize she'd made a terrible mistake.

"His heart finally gave out," Mama answered. "We knew he'd been getting weaker the past months, but I guess we didn't know how weak. He and Ma had their hot toddy as usual at bedtime last night. He told Ma he loved her before falling asleep and he never woke up."

I dressed in a daze and stumbled down the stairs behind Mama.

A silence heavy enough to suffocate a person hung over Ma's house all morning. By late afternoon Ma had washed Da and dressed him properly; the family men and old time boarders had laid him out in the parlor in a casket delivered by the best cabinetmaker in town, so they promised Ma. Soon the priest arrived for Da's wake and after that friends and neighbors streamed through the kitchen door with sandwiches and cakes. Then Da's friend, Mr. Murphy, arrived with two large bottles of Irish whiskey from his pub, and Uncle Jim and Uncle Danny poured drinks for the men and some of the women.

Mama and Bessie made tea and laid out the food on the dining table, stopping barely long enough to let themselves be hugged and kissed by the four cronies. I was amazed at how all the women carried on, greeting new arrivals as though they actually expected the world to keep right on spinning tomorrow. Even Ma, who loved Da more than her own life, passed around the sugar and creamer to the tea drinkers. Being too stunned to help out, I hid behind doors or on the back stairs most of the day until someone missed me and called out my name.

Hours went by and still I hadn't had the courage to visit Da in his casket. But once the mourners had wandered into the dining room and kitchen to tell stories and howl at their own jokes and say grand things about Grandpa William, I grabbed my opportunity. Dragging my feet down the hall to the parlor, heart racing, palms sweaty, insides icy cold, I felt my way through the candlelit room with my eyes squeezed shut until I reached the casket.

Forcing my eyes to open I gazed down at Da, sweet and handsome as ever, hands linked together, arms folded across his vest and watch chain, and suddenly I forgot to be afraid. I leaned forward within a few inches of his face and blubbered, tears dripping down my cheeks into my mouth and onto his beautiful reddish brown and gray beard. "I'll promise not to be sad, even when they lower you into your grave at the cemetery tomorrow," I whispered. "If you'll keep watching over me same as usual, taking my side and telling me I'm brave whether it's true or not."

I held his watch chain in my fist one last time. "And don't you worry about me for one minute. I'll know you'll be nearby when I need you—just like I know you can hear me now. And this will be our secret forever."

Then I brought two fingers to my mouth, licked them and set them gently on his lips. "So, no need to say goodbye, is there, Grandpa William?"

I gave one last look before leaving and went to the back of the house. I squeezed in next to the cronies at the kitchen table and Molly reached her arm around my shoulders while Liddy poured me a cup of tea.

Six weeks later, there was still an empty space next to my heart where Da used to live. The day Miss Campbell called out to me in the hallway between classes I wished I'd been invisible. I wasn't ready to greet anybody with a smile, much less a teacher yelling: "Stop, Ruthie. Stop!"

Then suddenly I heard Miss Campbell shout, "You won!" and I whipped myself around to face her and stomp my foot on the floorboard.

"No, I didn't," I said firmly. "Who really won?"

Next thing, I saw Miss Deasy tripping down the hall, eyes aglitter, mouth open wide. "I hear you won, Ruthie." She kept saying it so I knew it had to be true. Miss Deasy would never joke about a thing as important as this. When she reached me, she thrust an arm around my shoulder and gave me a squeeze. "I'm so proud of you. So proud." She arched her shoulders and gulped a mouthful of air. "They must have put a few Irish on the panel for a change."

In my head, I said, "Oh, my God, Da. Do you hear them? We won!" I kept repeating this in my head.

Or maybe I said it out loud because Miss Deasy said, "My, wouldn't your Grandpa William be proud of you!"

One week later, I felt more excited about beating out all those college students than about picking up my prize of six middy blouses. When I arrived at Getz Department Store, the contest sponsor, four sales ladies wearing long black dresses with stiff white collars greeted me at the front door. The women escorted me promptly into Ladies' Apparel, where a surprise party, red, white and blue balloons hanging from rafters and refreshments, awaited me.

A photographer from the *Mining Journal* popped a flash picture of me accepting the prize from the store manager for the Sunday newspaper. I certainly hadn't expected such a fuss; I'd planned to dash in, grab my prize and race home. Naturally, though, every inch of me tingled with the thrill of the event. The excitement, however, had my stomach turning somersaults. I couldn't possibly swallow the beautiful chocolate cake and strawberry ice cream they were serving, but the manager wrapped a huge piece of cake in a napkin and filled a paper bucket with ice cream for me to take home. Anxious to show off my prize to the family and boarders, I ran all five blocks back to Ma's house.

"They're beautiful," I said pulling on one of the blouses, then gazed down at where my chest should have rounded out to fill up the sagging white material under the navy blue sash.

Ma smiled ear to ear, but Mama noted my disappointment. "Don't worry, Ruthie, you'll grow into the blouses long before the six of them wear out," she said.

I giggled. "Sure? Then, that's more good news when I'm already the luckiest girl in town."

Mama and I both laughed hard, and Ma kept on smiling.

"You're getting too smart for your britches," Mama said that night before we got in bed, but her eyes were shining with pride. When we had both been under our quilt for some time, she touched my arm. "Are you awake, Ruthie?"

"Yeah. I'm too excited to sleep."

"Me too," she said. "You know Ma has always expected you to quit school at fifteen to go to work. Same as I did. I've been lying here praying for a miracle that would let you finish high school."

"I don't expect any miracles, Mama. Still, I was praying for the same thing." Although Mama and I—especially Mama—had worked for our keep every day of our lives, we felt beholden to Ma for letting us live with her all these years. Where else could a single mother and her child have gone? "Maybe two prayers for the same thing will count more than one alone," I said, trying to sound hopeful for Mama. "What do you think?"

"I think we have to get on our hands and knees and beg Ma to give you two more years board free." She patted my head. "Let's go to sleep now. We'll have to summon our courage and talk to Ma tomorrow when you get home from school. No good putting it off."

I reached for Mama's hand as we entered the kitchen where Ma was tending to the carrots and cabbage boiling on the stove. We both swallowed hard and Mama started in the way we had planned up in our room. "So much has changed for Ruthie since she began high school, don't you think, Ma? She's always had good report cards, but now, with the grace of God, she's become a prize-winning student as well." Ma kept stirring her vegetables with one hand and sprinkling salt and pepper over them with the other.

"She's already signed herself up for eleventh grade college preparatory courses. The point is, Ma, she wants to finish high school. And I want her to finish too."

Ma turned away from the stove and looked us in the face. "I'm not deaf and blind, Barbara. I know she's a smart girl with promise. Beyond this." She swung her arms in a half circle to encompass the entire kitchen. "Don't you think I'd have her graduate high school and go to college if there was any way on God's earth that were possible?" Ma brushed her cheek with the back of her hand and I had to look away to hide my astonishment. I'd never seen Ma cry; I didn't even know she *could* cry.

Mama ran to Ma's side and grabbed her hand. "Let Ruthie graduate. We'll manage somehow for a couple of more years. She'll take care of herself after that."

"What kind of job can she get if she takes only courses for college?" Ma wiped her palm across her forehead. "A woman has to stand up for herself. I've tried to teach her that. I don't want her doing hard labor like the rest of us. I want her to get a decent job requiring skills in an office where she can hold her head up and dress nice every day."

"Then I'll take the business course instead of college preparatory," I said. "I can take writing and literature courses for extra credit. I can do it, Ma. I promise, if you let me finish high school." I couldn't seem to breathe right; I kept watching her mouth waiting for the words that might change my life.

Ma walked over to the table, dropped into a chair, and turned to Mama. "I'd take in ten more boarders if I could let her finish high school and ten more after that to send her to the University in Ann Arbor, but we'd have to hang them from the rafters."

"I know," Mama said.

Ma looked at me long and hard. "You would have to keep your word, Ruthie." She pinched her lips together and kept her hand to her forehead before continuing. "If you think you can take all those courses at once I'll think of some way to manage for another two years."

For half a second I thought about running over to her and hugging her, but by then she had already hurried back to the stove where steam was rising from the vegetable pot, so I said real quick, "Thank you, Ma. I'll never forget this."

More than half the students in my sophomore class had to get fulltime jobs at the end of the school year. Since they couldn't remain in high school for the last two years, the school honored them with an evening ceremony of their own in June of that year. I helped write the class prophesies and read them from the auditorium stage on the night of the occasion. I guess they were funny, cause the kids giggled and doubled over and slapped each on the back, but all the while I felt a little sad inside.

When I got into bed that night, I thanked God again for allowing me to continue in high school. Luckily, Brendan who would be a senior, Teresa, Myrtle and Louisa would be coming back in the fall with me. But Olive had already dropped out mid-year to take a job waitressing in a restaurant downtown, and Maggie was to start work as a housekeeper the next week in one of the grand homes on Ridge Street.

One afternoon that summer I happened to meet Miss Deasy downtown in front of Kresge's Dime Store. "You're going to enjoy the college prep classes next year, Ruthie," she said setting one hand on my shoulder. "And do very well, I'm sure."

Miss Deasy had been the first to drag my secret talent into the light of day and to encourage me to use it. I dreaded telling her that I'd had to switch curriculums, so I spit it out fast to get it over with. "I'm enrolled in business courses now."

She frowned in a way that displayed no anger and picked up my hand. "I see. I guess I know why. I understand and I'm so sorry." She gave my hand a gentle squeeze. "I've been looking into future possibilities for you all this year. I hope you don't mind. There are some teacher and nurse state scholarships here at State Normal College, but that's about it. Seems impossible to get tuition and living expense scholarships for girls, downstate or anywhere, for that matter, who want to pursue other studies."

"Thank you for trying. You didn't have to do that," I told her. She kept my hand in hers, so I didn't move. "There's no way to send me off to college, Miss Deasy. I never expected that. I have to get a job after high school to start paying room and board to my Grandma Bridget. Also, Mama can't marry her engineer fella or anybody else until I'm earning my own living. She doesn't say that, but I know. And she deserves to be happy."

"I know your Mama. She's proud of you. Her dreams would be answered if you could go away to college."

"That's a dream, all right. Anyway, I'm glad Ma let me stay in school another two years. I'll be the first girl in our family to finish high school. Ma says that's an honor in itself."

"Of course it is."

I kept hold of Miss Deasy's hand. Now it was me that didn't want to let go. "I'm going to take some pre-college classes during the next two years. I figure that later I can take composition and writing courses at State Normal college on my day off from work. And I plan to enroll in literature classes after that. So, you see, I've been doing some research too."

"My, how you've grown up in the past year, girl." At last Miss Deasy smiled. "Watching you from my parlor window sailing down our hill on the front end of those bobsleds the past few years, is enough to convince me that you'll accomplish whatever you set out to do."

"You saw me? And you never told Ma or Mama?"

"And spoil your fun? No."

"Be sure to watch this winter then. I'm being promoted to an actual team member at the back end."

Miss Deasy shook her head and chuckled. "Call me anytime I can help with your studies." She released my hand. "Be sure, Ruthie."

Though I had dreaded telling Miss Deasy my change of plans, I felt only relief as I watched her walk away.

My mind lept from idea to idea all the way home from downtown. What's the use of having talent beyond bringing in the cows and performing stunts that could kill me, if I ignore my "gift," as Mama called it? I wouldn't write milk soppy pieces, though, like those printed in magazines for girls and women. I'd want to write stories about real people who had trouble feeding their families, and did what they needed to do to survive. Even when it meant sending young daughters and sons out to work in dangerous places, while having more and more children at home to take care of. And I'd like to write about men who crossed oceans and carried families across continents to have a better life, and about those who failed to measure up to the task and took to the drink and lost their wives and children. And I'd hope to write about the slow children who got kicked around and were never taught anything worthwhile. And about people who spit into the wind because the wind has never been at their backs. And yet found much to laugh about and to enjoy. And who go on thanking the powers that be for being where they are which is still better than where they came from.

Epilogue

I DID WHAT I had promised myself and Mama and Ma that I would do. I passed all the commercial classes with flying colors, got honor points in the extra college preparatory courses that I loved and finished school in 1918. The hardest part of those two years was saying goodbye to Brendan who had graduated the year before me and left for the University of Michigan in September, then only a few months later enlisted in the army and was sent off to Europe to fight in the World War to end all wars.

I found a job in the office of a home loan company where I could dress nice every day and that pleased Mama. She gave me the once over at breakfast each morning to make sure I looked like a proper working girl before leaving home. Having finished school, I was already well ahead of all the women in my family who had come before me. And that fall I planned to attend college courses after work each afternoon. This meant I would never have to do service in other people's homes, scrubbing and cleaning them and taking care of their children. And also, I was proud to collect a paycheck every Saturday and pay Ma room and board.

Most days I brought a sandwich from home and ate at my desk, but one day a week I allowed myself the luxury of having lunch at Walgreen's. One gray January day like any other, I buttoned my heavy wool coat to the neck and braced myself against a sharp edged wind swirling up Washington Street and slapping me in the face. I had barely had a chance to set down my glass of milk and ham salad sandwich when the most extraordinary thing happened. A tall handsome soldier, obviously just returned from the war and still wearing his uniform, sat next to me at the counter. "Do you mind if I sit here?" he asked. "This seems to be the only vacant seat in the lunchroom." And this is how my courtship with Floyd Thomas began.

Tommy, as his friends called him, reminded me and all my friends of Brendan, or rather, Brendan, had Brendan been a few years older. Quick witted, fun loving Tommy was twenty-six. Full of ambition like Brendan, Tommy was bent on getting a degree in engineering, although he had no more means of attending college full-time than I did. In this, we became comrades, endlessly discussing our nearly impossible dreams. Five years and three children later, Tommy actually did sign up for night classes in engineering at Wayne University. Having worked nine hours a day as a tool and dye maker in a Detroit factory each day, he attended classes in the evening. Then, spreading his books out on a table in our tiny kitchen, he studied until the early A.M.

A few years later, however, almost to the day that Tommy received his cherished engineering diploma, Wall Street collapsed and the Great Depression swept across the country, Atlantic to Pacific, changing millions of lives overnight. People everywhere struggled just to keep their children from starving and to stay alive themselves. Finally we were able to move back to Marquette when, by some miracle, Tommy was offered a job managing the Munising Wood Products manufacturing plant.

By then, Willie had found Lempi, a fine Finnish girl, to marry. He'd been promoted by the railroad from popcorn butcher to laying ties. He and Lempi had a daughter who was so smart in school she was classified a genius. So, how's that for justice and things evening out in the end?

And Mama had fallen in love again. "Just as much in love as I was with Mr. Andrews back in 1912," she exclaimed. She married Charlie Ruggles, a Marquette boy, in 1921, soon after my own wedding in 1920. Charlie whisked her off to Lansing immediately where he had a steady accounting job. Mama thought she'd been transported to heaven on earth taking care of a mere two people in her very own home.

A few years after Mama's wedding, Bessie, never looking happier, married Claire Harrington, a handsome bachelor who had rented Ma's only single person room for about a year.

I managed to cling stubbornly to my own earlier dreams, although doing that seemed almost greedy while so many others were jobless, living in tents in hobo camps and sleeping in railroad cars. Still, I believe it was that kind of hope that got Tommy and me through the Depression. Often, late at night, we recited the old dreams aloud to each other so we wouldn't forget them.

Not a day went by, however, that I didn't marvel at how Ma and Mama and the rest of the folks at Ma's had persevered all those years with no conveniences to comfort them. Yet, they had never seemed *desperately* unhappy. I wondered if they had been appreciative of whatever they had, having had so much less earlier in their lives. Mama, however, had wanted more than Ma had and I had surely wanted more than Mama had. So Tommy and I refused to give up on the expectations we had for our family and ourselves even during the tough 1930's.

In the strange way things can work out, I decided later that my own childhood had prepared me more than many for the Depression. At Ma's house, I had learned to do without things that kids in another part of town took for granted. Coaxing a twenty-five cent pound of hamburger into feeding six people, or telling a child it wasn't his or her turn for new shoes, never mind that loose soles flapped on the pavement with each step he took, never seemed to forecast the end of the world to me. We felt fortunate to be living in a rented home with radiator heat and running hot water and an indoor bathroom, all things Ma and Mama, the rest of the family and our boarders would have considered grand luxuries.

Somehow during the hardest of times I managed to save enough coins each month to call Mama in Lansing. Hearing her voice was all I seemed to

need. One morning she told me, "Ruthie, you refused to be the sweet little girl Ma wanted. If you
survived Ma's wrath, believe me, you will be able
to survive tornadoes, earthquakes, hurricanes and
even this damn Depression." And I believed her.
After all, fortune had never tapped people at Ma's
house on their shoulders offering them golden opportunities. They'd had to chase them down like
starving wolverines pursuing unsuspecting prey.
So, I knew one way or another that things would
get better.

Then, just in time, it would seem, President
Franklin Delano Roosevelt's grand plans for the
country gave everybody the courage to hope and
permission to dream again. So, lo and behold, I
woke up one morning and realized that Tommy
and I and our family had somehow managed to
outlast the Depression.

No matter what was happening in my own life
at the time, though, I never once stopped wondering what had become of Papa. I'd spent half of my
childhood, it seemed, telling lies about him to my
friends and the other half defending him and the
Hogans from Ma's fierce tongue. I hadn't seen him
for more than twenty years, not since 1910 back
when he'd shown up at Vangie Pelisier's news shack
that blizzardy afternoon. Then one morning, Aunt
Nellie Hogan called me, voice high pitched and excited. "Dommy's back, Ruthie," she said, "He'll be
in town all week! He's looking grand. Been working
steady setting presses at a newspaper in Chicago
and on the wagon for a year this time."

"Good," I sputtered with the shock of his reappearance beginning to sink in. "Tell him it's okay if he wants to visit me."

My father, gray and brown beard trimmed, cheeks gleaming with a brand new wash, hair freshly cut, arrived at our home on Alger Street in a borrowed car the next evening. A minute later he stood in our vestibule wearing a suit, slightly shiny in the seat but well pressed by his sister Nellie. "You're looking lovely, Ruthie," he said.

I walked over to him and set a hand on his arm. "Come in and meet your grandchildren," I said, directing him into the front room. The children inspected the stranger before them with curious eyes as I introduced each one, Billy, seven, Jean, six, and Shirley, five, to their grandpa.

"You've done all right," Papa said while following me into the kitchen.

Should I tell him about the years at Ma's house, feeling like nobody's or everybody's child, having an old fashioned, mean at times, grandmother ordering Mama and me around, every one of us working day and night to take care of all those boarders? Or, should I pour salt in the wound by relating the happy times, telling him how much I loved Da, my sweet Grandpa William? What was the point of either, though, I wondered. Why increase his guilt, if he had any, or feed his sorrow over what he himself had missed?

Then he touched my shoulder gently like someone who hadn't a right and asked if he could see our new baby.

"Of course," I said. Replacing the lid on a pot of freshly mashed potatoes, I led him into our bedroom where an infant slept peacefully in a bassinette next to our bed.

He placed his hand on the white wicker cradle. "And what is her name?" he asked.

Reaching down to straighten the baby's quilt, part of me wanting to answer, another part of me hesitating, I answered finally. "Barbara," I said.

"After your mother, of course," he said lowering himself to the bed to get a closer look. Mama left the room but Papa didn't return to the kitchen for several minutes.

Fortunately, Tommy arrived home from work a few minutes later and kept the conversation at the table jaunting along from the woodenware business to baseball, to another writing class I was taking at the college and to the children who to my surprise were behaving as if having their grandad Dominic seated at our table was a very ordinary occurrence.

Soon Papa warmed up and started to tell lively stories regarding his past "gypsy life," as he called it, the constant moves and renting furnished places on their last legs that were inhabited by vagabonds like himself barely scratching out a living. Somehow, the way he described things, though, his life didn't sound the least bit pitiful. In fact, he kept us laughing till the end of the meal. Then, as though he didn't want the evening to be overwith, he asked Tommy if we would follow him back to the Fisher House for tea with Aunt Nellie.

"Let's go. Please Mom, Dad?" yelped Billy, his sister Jean echoing him and younger sister Shirley squealing about how much she loved going to Aunt Nellie's.

Aunt Nellie, having welcomed us at the door, set about preparing tea and serving us fresh butter cookies on a living room side table. Then, dropping her ample frame onto a piano bench, inquired, "Well, if this isn't an excuse for a party, what is?"

Papa gulped down his tea and gathering the kids around him at the piano announced, "I'll lead," Using his teaspoon as a baton he directed the children's singing—or humming when they didn't know the words—through song after song.

Sneaking glances at fifty-seven-year old Papa's startling blue eyes and easy smile, I caught a glimpse of the young man my mother, just a girl herself, had fallen in love with. Holding my baby on my lap, I listened proudly to my children's voices as Papa encouraged them. He gave me a pleased sideways glance every so often, then winked and grinned at me. "Maybe the Hogan musical talent was only dormant for a generation, Ruthie," he said.

On the porch as we were leaving, Papa gave each of the children a dime for firecrackers to use at our Fourth of July celebration a few days off. Then, as naturally as if this were a weekly event, he bent down and kissed each of them, even the baby, on the cheek and said goodnight to them.

The very next day, Mama happened to arrive in town for a visit with Ma and a few of the boarders who had stayed on to help Ma with expenses. Mama and I met each other downtown on Wash-

ington Street. We were busy pushing baby Barbara
in her buggy and catching up on Ma's married life
in Lansing when I looked up and, then and there,
saw Papa strolling right down the street toward us.
A second later, before I had a chance to faint, he
was near enough for me to touch him and he caught
my eye. As if time stood still, I held my breath and
waited for him to speak. I decided later that he'd
probably been waiting for Mama to acknowledge
him and when Mama said nothing, he walked on by
without uttering a word. A great wave of sadness
washed over me when I realized that after all these
years Mama hadn't even recognized her Dominic
and worst of all, he had realized she hadn't.

When he was safely past us, I asked Mama,
"Do you know who that was?"

"You mean the nice looking man in the cap?
Should I?"

"That was my father," I said.

Mama stopped and, turning discreetly, watched
him walk away.

"We saw him last night. I planned to tell you all
about it as soon as we sat down to tea in Donker's
Ice Cream Parlor.

"Oh, my," she said, tightening her fingers to the
buggy handle, the other hand smoothing her flowered print cotton dress, then touching her bobbed
brunette hair streaked with gray now. "Well, I'm
certainly glad I dressed up nice today."

"You look beautiful, Mama. Just beautiful," I
assured her.

She gave my hand a squeeze. "You think so?" she said with a toss of her head and a sudden spring to her step.

That was the last time I saw my father. He left town the next day. I suppose coming back to town had been hard for him, seeing what he had lost, or what he'd been denied, however he viewed the cause of his being cut off from his family for all those years. Or perhaps he regretted having protected himself from hurt by staying away. I would never know which applied. All I knew was that he'd never remarried; he'd worked off and on, but never stayed in one place long enough to make a stable life for himself.

Years after his visit, Aunt Nellie called me one morning, and with a choked voice, told me, "Dommy died yesterday. His current landlady rang us up with the news that he'd dropped dead yesterday from a stroke on a Chicago street. He was seventy-five two months ago, you know. Good thing our sister Lizzie has moved back into the Fisher Street house with me. She's still young enough to take a train to Chicago to attend the funeral. His landlady said he would be buried in Catholic churchyard cemetery."

Nellie started to sob at the other end, but since I didn't know how I felt, I could only tell her to fix herself some tea and I would try to come see her later in the day. The news didn't seem real to me for several hours. I guess I'd assumed that old Dommy would be out there somewhere roaming the earth forever.

Ma called me as soon as she heard about his passing. "It was probably a pauper's grave," she stated as though she had personally received this information from a Higher Authority.

I called Mama as soon as Ma hung up. "Age hasn't sweetened Ma's tongue any," Mama said when I repeated Ma's words. "Ma doesn't know any such thing," Mama said, then paused. "Although I suppose it is true."

Not long after Papa died, a feature story appeared in the *Milwaukee Sentinel* newspaper that cheered me up some regarding Papa. *The Sentinel* ran a series about ancient train robberies, and the old South Shore Railroad robbery in Marquette, sixty years earlier, was among them. Most of the newspaper story was about Dominic's big brother Ed, the con man and planner of the heist. The reporter's investigation exposed Ed's underhanded treatment of Dommy and how he'd talked his younger brother into confessing and taking the rap. The *Sentinal* writer also revealed the truth he'd unearthed about how Ed had buried the loot in a cave up in the Copper Country the first night they were on the lam while Dommy slept under a tree.

"'Lucky Eddie,' invested his booty in lucrative oil stocks and never shared the earnings with his kid brother," the reporter wrote. "And Dominic never recovered from his anger at being cheated out of his share of profits from the crime or from the shame of serving time."

Growing up in Grandma Bridget and Grandpa William's house, everyone had expected me to be ashamed of my father, but that's not the way I felt. Secretly, I remained a little proud of him. For one thing, I thought he was more adventurous than the fathers of my friends, and besides, I could make up fabulous stories about him: at various times he was an officer in the Foreign Legion, a ship captain, a famous author—whatever struck me on that particular day. Nobody knew where my papa was any more than I did. I could tell people anything. Truth is, I'd always been angrier with Edward for keeping the entire booty for himself than I was ever ashamed of Papa.

In any case, the ancient train robberies story in *The Milwaukee Sentinel* ruined eighty-year old Edward's carefully cultivated image in his hometown, Marquette, as well as in the entire state of Minnesota where he still resided. I felt that this partly settled the score for Papa—Dominic's revenge in black and white for the whole world to read. I set the newspaper on our kitchen table and smiled to myself over the demise of Ed's reputation, certain in my heart that Dommy was doing the same, wherever he was.

AUTHOR'S NOTE

RUTH HOGAN THOMAS, "Ruthie," and her husband Floyd Thomas, "Tommy," raised six children in all. He continued to manage the woodenware manufacturing company and she took charge of a family business they had acquired: a deli, spirits and general shop. Their youngest child, Danny, was nine when his father died. Ruth, at forty-eight, Danny in tow, moved to Chicago and began a new career with United Air Lines. In her capacity as a traveling company representative for the United Air Lines Credit Union she worked in cities all across the United States through 1967.

During those years in Chicago, she read enthusiastically and took courses in communications at the University of Chicago. She continued to put pen to paper in her journal each evening creating the bulk of material for this memoir. She appeared in a contemporary women's discussion group on a Chicago public access television station on occasion and also attended political and anti-war rallies with me, her daughter Barbara, during the late sixties and early seventies.

After retiring from United Air Lines, she moved back to Marquette and into an apartment building where some of her childhood friends and original members of "the music club," widowed and single again themselves, also lived. Together, and with some new members, they reassembled themselves under the name "The Marquette Merry Music Makers." Wearing old time costumes and large flower decorated hats, they played gigs at the new shopping mall, the Veterans' Hospital, nursing homes, a supper club and on the back of a flat bed truck in every parade that marched down Washington Street on holidays.

During her retirement years, Ruth finished writing her personal remembrances of the past. In her eighties, she gave me all of her journals with a request that I turn them into a story and call it *Dominic's Daughter*. "Because I don't think I'll have time to finish the job myself," she said.

Ruth Hogan Thomas, enjoyed those last years, living independently, traveling abroad to places she'd only dreamed about in her upstairs bedroom at Ma's boarding house and visiting her six children scattered throughout America. Smart, witty and spunky as ever, "Ruthie" died at age eighty-nine in the arms of Kathleen, one of her granddaughters. All six of her children, their wives and husbands and sixteen grandchildren celebrated her wake in a grand old riotous Hogan fashion that would have made her ever so proud.

ABOUT THE AUTHOR

Barbara Mullen

ARBARA (THOMAS) MUL-
LEN was born and grew
up in Marquette, a small
town in the upper peninsula of
Michigan. She graduated from
Northern Michigan University
with a bachelor's degree in so-
ciology and spent four years
in the United States Foreign Serivce in Southeast
Asia and Japan.

In 1960, she married William Mullen, a Marine
Corps lieutenant. They had two young sons, Sean
and Terence, when Lt. Mullen's plane was shot
down in 1966 during the Vietnam War. In 1970,
Barbara Mullen founded Families for Immediate
Release, a national POW/MIA wives organization
that lobbied to end the war.

Barbara earned a master's degree in creative
writing from Lesley College in 1985 and since then
has published two books, *Every Effort*, St Martin's
Press, and *When You Marry a Man with Children*,
Pocket Books, Simon & Schuster. Her freelance
articles have appeared in *The Boston Herald*, *The
Cape Cod Times*, and *Sojourner*.

She now lives in the San Francisco Bay Area near her two sons. She has four grandsons, Wiliam, Christopher, Edward, and Fynnigan.

Printed in the United States
49942LVS00001B/27